The Professional's
Guide to Fair Value

Founded in 1807, John Wiley & Sons is the oldest independent publishing company in the United States. With offices in North America, Europe, Asia, and Australia, Wiley is globally committed to developing and marketing print and electronic products and services for our customers' professional and personal knowledge and understanding.

The Wiley Corporate F&A series provides information, tools, and insights to corporate professionals responsible for issues affecting the profitability of their companies, from accounting and finance to internal controls and performance management.

The Professional's Guide to Fair Value

The Future of Financial Reporting

JAMES P. CATTY

WILEY

John Wiley & Sons, Inc.

Published by John Wiley & Sons, Inc., Hoboken, New Jersey.
Published simultaneously in Canada.

For general information on our other products and services or for technical support, please contact our Customer Care Department within the United States at (800) 762-2974, outside the United States at (317) 572-3993 or fax (317) 572-4002.

Wiley also publishes its books in a variety of electronic formats. Some content that appears in print may not be available in electronic books. For more information about Wiley products, visit our web site at www.wiley.com.

Library of Congress Cataloging-in-Publication Data:

Catty, James P.
 The professional's guide to fair value : the future of financial reporting / James P. Catty.
  p. cm. -- (Wiley corporate F&A series)
 Includes index.
  ISBN 978-1-118-00438-8 (hardback); ISBN 978-1-118-18542-1 (ebk); ISBN 978-1-118-18543-8 (ebk); ISBN 978-1-118-18544-5 (ebk)
 1. Fair value--Accounting--Standards. 2. Financial statements. I. Title.
 HF5681.V3C37 2012
 657'.3--dc23

                                                      2011034184

10 9 8 7 6 5 4 3 2 1

To Dita, who prevents life becoming un huis clos

Contents

Preface

What's a cynic? A man who knows the price of
everything and the value of nothing.

—Oscar Fingal O'Flahertie Wilde (1854–1900), Irish author

O N JULY 4, 1956, over 55 years ago, I arrived in New York on the *Queen Mary*; it was the sixteenth anniversary of my first of numerous visits to the United States. The trip was part of a summer job as a junior securities analyst, visiting steel companies in the United States and Europe; this was an essential element of a project to compare the values of the publicly traded shares of recently denationalized British steel companies with their stock market prices. While an interesting, indeed fascinating, endeavor, it was not profitable for the London stockbroker who initiated it, as nearly all the shares were overvalued, but at that time few institutional investors were willing to sell or switch. Today, there are no publicly traded shares of British steel companies; the major producer is now Tata Steel Europe, wholly Indian-owned.

This long-ago experience convinced me that value is something connected to, but not necessarily the same as, price, even though the Financial Accounting Standards Board (FASB) in the United States and the International Accounting Standards Board (IASB) in the rest of the world have justifiably based their concept of fair value for financial reporting on the price a seller could receive for an item. This is the subject of the book; it is not designed for specialist valuation experts or even for neophytes in the profession I have practiced, seemingly forever, seeking the latest and greatest techniques. My aim is to assist other professionals—lawyers, accountants, teachers, bankers, judges, investors, analysts, and managers—in their dealings with fair value.

The term *fair value* was first introduced in June 2001 by FASB in Statement of Financial Reporting Standards (SFAS) 141, *Business Combinations*, now Accounting Standards Codification (ASC) 805, and in SFAS 142, *Goodwill and Other Intangible Assets*, now ASC 350. For the past 10 years, I have been concerned with the concept (my wife would say obsessed), and have written and presented about it extensively. Over that period, fair value has become increasingly important in business and finance. Every entity, whether a corporation, trust, partnership, limited or unlimited company, even a proprietorship, is likely to have at least one asset on its balance sheet that is recorded using it.

May 12, 2011, was a red-letter day for everyone concerned with fair value or indeed with financial reporting. On that date, FASB issued a revision of ASC 820, *Fair Value Measurements*, and IASB announced International Financial Reporting Standard (IFRS) 13, *Fair Value Measurement*. Those virtually identical documents gave the financial world a single definition and framework in this area, uniting Generally Accepted Accounting Principles (GAAP) in the United States and IFRS, thus making this book possible.

Today's expanding global business environment demands that all professionals responsible for financial information must work together, helping one another and relying on each other. Accountants, auditors, and appraisers (valuators) must ensure that every stakeholder in an entity—management, owners, creditors and regulators—receive reliable, up-to-date financial information to fulfill their needs, duties, and responsibilities. Data must be accurately recorded, valued, and audited. Errors at any stage will lead to incorrect, or even damaging, decisions. With the expansion of IFRS, the roles of accountants and auditors are becoming harmonized; now is the era of the valuator.

Management needs to know, in detail, the costs involved in producing, selling, and distributing the entity's various goods and services, and must ensure that there are enough funds available for capital expenditures and working capital and to provide shareholders with the dividends that ensure continuing investment.

Owners need such material to decide whether to buy or sell securities, to establish their trading prices, as well as to measure portfolio performance and volatility. Today, investors have many choices, and reliable financial information is the fundamental underpinning for their decisions. Creditors, including banks and suppliers, need this material for practical, rational decisions about a firm's ability to pay its bills and to properly service both its short-term and long-term obligations. Lenders use the information when deciding to make new loans, extend existing ones, or enhance lines of credit. Vendors rely on it to grant trade credit and enter into long-term contracts. Last, but not least, regulators insist on reliable financial information as part of their duty to protect the public trust.

Accountants deal mostly with the present, recording every activity of the entity. Auditors, who are trained as accountants, deal with the past, confirming that the financial statements present fairly the results of preceding activities. Valuators look to the future, calculating what someone will pay now for benefits that are yet to come; they perform their services and reach their conclusions based on information and data from the entity's accountants and advice from its auditors. Those services and conclusions may include determining the fair value of: a whole firm; an individual division, subsidiary, or department; specific financial, physical, or intangible assets; or a potential acquisition target.

Valuing individual assets, especially items of intellectual property, is essential to the impairment tests required by GAAP and IFRS to be applied to long-lived assets and goodwill at least once a year. Through its accountants, management provides accurate, up-to-date financial material and operating information to the valuators; the latter then give the accountants their value conclusions to be incorporated into the books and records of the entity, so that they can be blessed by the auditors. A properly conducted valuation engagement must be able to rely on the financial material and operating information; the quality of the conclusion is adversely affected by inaccurate or inadequate inputs.

Any and all users, regulators, practitioners, or educators concerned with valuations, wherever located, should make themselves completely familiar with all the matters discussed in this book. It, and my previous works, including *Guide to Fair Value under IFRS* (John Wiley & Sons, 2010), should help all of us achieve uniformity and consistency in our endeavors in the field. This is especially important due to the current convergences in financial reporting, as well as the consolidation of business through mergers, acquisitions, and restructurings, and the changing availability of financing worldwide.

Toronto, Canada
January 2012

Acknowledgments

TO WRITE A BOOK is a complicated endeavor. Having gone that route before, I know the importance of partners, colleagues, and associates. Therefore I would like to thank my partner in business and life, Dita Vadron, for her unfailing support. Thanks also to my colleagues in the International Association of Consultants, Valuators and Analysts: Susan Yi in China; James Horvath and Zareer Pavri in Canada; and Wolfgang Kniest, Robert Brackett, Richard Claywell, William A. Hanlin Jr., and Terry Isom in the United States for unfailing support and useful comments. Without the helpful staff at John Wiley & Sons and my invaluable assistant, Hellen Cumber, this opus would never have seen the light of day.

CHAPTER ONE

Significance of Value

It's always hard to value things. In some cases, you don't have enough information. In other cases, you don't want to know the truth.

—*Donald Brownstein (1972–), American investor*

S INCE THE BEGINNING OF TIME, some form of valuation has been involved in estimating the worth or price of each item in every exchange between trading parties. Whether through barter, cash, or some other medium, assets have been exchanged constantly in personal, business, and taxation transactions on some agreed-on basis. Before money and banks, payments often consisted of sheep, goats, or bushels of grain; in each case, an implicit value was involved. As a result, based on the earliest known records, from around 5000 B.C. at Jericho in Israel, some consider valuation to be the world's fifth oldest profession, after hunters, farmers, merchants, and priests.

BUSINESS USES FOR VALUATION

When considering a substantial business deal, whether a major expansion, significant acquisition, plant closure, or considerable divestiture, management will eventually reach a tipping point. A go/no-go decision has to be made, based on a bottom line calculated from inadequate information. The key questions are: How much value will be created, and for whom? The answers can be elusive; the process is rather like trying to distinguish a black sock from a blue one when dressing in the dark. Often, many of the assets involved can't be seen and aren't recorded anywhere, but are still real.

Many readers, be they lawyers, accountants, teachers, bankers, judges, investors, analysts, or managers, will have had some involvement with the valuation process. They will know how challenging it is to determine the value of a business asset. But some may not realize the difficulties and may still look at traditional accounting statements to show how much a company or even an asset is worth. Please don't! Those figures are generally based on historical costs, after some amortization, and reflect the past, not the present.

In reality, value is about the future; it is also about many more assets than the traditional items—receivables; inventory; property, plant & equipment—beloved of bankers, that we all can touch and feel. Much of the value of any company, as seen by purchasers and investors, lies in its unrecorded, usually internally generated, intangible assets—brands, licenses, contracts, workforce expertise, and so forth. Some authorities place the figure for the United States at over 70%, as shown by the Standard & Poor's (S&P) 500 index. The existence of intangible assets makes the art of the deal somewhat like trying to put a key in the front door lock when the porch light is off.

When a business buys a building for $2 million, it shows the same amount as an asset on its balance sheet and has it available as collateral for borrowing. If it hires an employee who is brilliant and can generate an additional $3 million in sales, with a guaranteed bonus of $300,000, the firm not only cannot record an asset, but must show the guaranteed payment as a liability. Yet the purchase of the building is likely to add less to the fair value of the firm than the additional profits and cash flows generated by the hiring.

MERGERS AND ACQUISITIONS

The most obvious need for valuators in business comes when a merger or an acquisition is undertaken. If the buyer is strategic, its managers often wonder how much of that very intangible asset popularly known as synergy will be generated by the transaction. What effect should it have on the price they are willing to pay? There is obvious value, perhaps a significant amount, in immediately being able to use otherwise idle productive capacity or to have direct access to new products or markets. However, there are also always risks and costs involved, sometimes considerable ones. Both the advantages and the risks are things management must question and a valuator has to quantify. For the increasing number of financial buyers, valuation is even more important. What can be paid often depends on which noncore assets can be sold and for how much.

 ## FINANCIAL REPORTING

Since the 2008–2009 worldwide financial crisis, when many financial markets ceased to function effectively, and the resulting recession, more and more attention is being paid to corporate financial reporting. International Financial Reporting Standards (IFRS) have been or are being adopted by over 100 countries, representing more than half of the market capitalization of every stock market in the world. The main holdout is the United States, which has always believed in the sanctity of its own highly developed Generally Accepted Accounting Principles (GAAP). However, their custodian, the Financial Accounting Standards Board (FASB), is continuing to work with the International Accounting Standards Board (IASB), creators of IFRS, to harmonize the two regimes. Happily, the integration of the two accounting languages is not likely to lead to a mishmash franglais, as exemplified by *"Donnez-moi les* cornflakes"—"Pass me the cornflakes." The major impact will likely be a level playing field around the financial world, with more assets being reported at fair values as against historical costs.

During the first decade of the 2000s there were significant changes in financial reporting in the United States. One major improvement was a change in accounting for acquisitions and the attendant introduction of goodwill impairment testing. Under both GAAP and IFRS it is now mandatory for all acquirers to allocate the purchase price of a target among the various assets acquired—financial, physical, and intangible—as well as the liabilities assumed, in keeping with their fair values. In general, all long-lived assets, except goodwill, which is an unamortized residual that is only tested for impairment, have to be amortized, thus impacting earnings.

Intangible Assets

To be recognized as an asset, an intangible must satisfy one of two criteria: it must be either contractual in nature or salable. As the purchase price allocation (PPA) process is critical to most transactions (see Chapter 13), valuators have gradually taken on a more strategic role in the acquisition process. They help identify potential intangible assets that may be owned by the target, and develop preliminary views as to their values during the planning, regulatory approval, and due diligence phases. Although any residual is booked as goodwill and not amortized, it, together with all long-lived physical and intangible assets, has to be annually tested for impairment. This is done to determine whether any reductions of carrying amounts are required as a result of changed circumstances. While only purchased intangible assets are recorded, the key Step 2 of the GAAP goodwill impairment test that determines the amount of any write-off does not differentiate between them and similar internally generated items.

Fair Value Measurement

In plain language, fair value is a broad concept; a thesaurus gives 47 synonyms for *fair*, including candid, equitable, honest, impartial, just, lawful, plain, reasonable, sincere, and upright. Without the modifier *market*, fair value can be seen as a "value" that is "fair." Accordingly, there is wide latitude as to what it might be. Depending on circumstances, the fair value of an asset could be its market, intrinsic, or investment value and might represent either a liquidation or a going-concern amount. Fortunately, FASB and IASB have developed a fixed definition, which is discussed in Chapter 2, and a related framework to estimate it, described in Chapter 3.

Fair Market Value

The term *fair market value*, which can be traced back to *United States v. Fourteen Packages of Pins*, an 1832 federal court tariff case, has become well defined and fully established in legal, tax, and accounting settings. It now relates to finding the value that an asset would have on a market that is fair, in the context of a real or hypothetical sale.

From the mid-nineteenth century onward, with the development of national and then international markets, the need for business valuation in most Western countries has been driven principally by insurance and tax/tariff requirements. In recent years the focus has moved to fair value for financial reporting. In the United States the term was used, interchangeably with fair market value, during the 1920s to record assets on balance sheets. In 1933, the newly minted Securities and Exchange Commission (SEC), due to the excessive share price declines since 1929, prohibited any write-ups of assets over their original cost.

At the same time, the SEC switched the emphasis among the financial statements from the balance sheet (statement of financial position) to that for profit and loss (income statement or statement of operations); we are now seeing a form of "back to the future" as the emphasis is gradually returning to assets and liabilities from revenues and expenses—but that is another story.

Relevant Documents

Fast-forward 20 years to 1953; the Depression is long over, prosperity is back, and fair value returns. In that year, Accounting Research Bulletin (ARB) 43 stated that from then on, fair value was to be the basis for recording all assets acquired in a purchase; however, the term was not defined, nor were any procedures prescribed to estimate it.

The 1970s, in the aftermath of some so-called "dirty pooling" scandals, saw the issuance of Accounting Principles Board (APB) Opinions 16 and 17. Under them, fair value was again required to be used in recording assets acquired other than in a pooling of interests. They also established the notion of identifying and recording purchased intangible assets, apart from goodwill; for fair value, this was the beginning of the modern era. As none of those terms were defined, the tradition arose of using the same fair market values for recognizing assets on the financial statements as were shown on the tax returns; any unallocated balance went to goodwill, which was amortized over a period of up to 40 years.

Then came the booming 1990s, when economic changes forced a new look at accounting policies. In that decade, there were numerous, sometimes enormous, acquisitions fueled by new technologies and the apparent strength of firms' intangible assets and intellectual property. The latter is an important subset of intangible assets (patents, trademarks, copyrights, designs, trade secrets, etc.) that are granted specific legal protection.

The average price-to-book ratio of the S&P 500 index is considered a useful proxy for the unrecorded intangible assets owned by American industry. This rose from about 1.1 times in 1982, the start of the last major bull market in shares, to close to 5.0 times at the peak in 1999; it has since dropped to around 3.0 times in 2010.

In that so-called Goldilocks era (1990–2005), when growth of the U.S. economy was not too big, but not too small, a significant number of FASB documents dealt with value, measurement methods, and present value techniques. Of the 32 Statements of Financial Accounting Standards (SFAS) issued in the decade, 15 addressed recognition or measurement issues, and 11, with some overlap, referred to present value techniques.

The first few years of the new millennium were hectic. In 2000, FASB issued Concept Statement 7 dealing with net present value as a means of estimating fair value. In June 2001, it issued SFAS 141 and SFAS 142, quickly followed by SFAS 144, *Accounting for the Impairment or Disposal of Long-Lived Assets*. Those documents included an earlier definition of fair value and provided detailed procedures for recording intangible assets in business combinations. The American Institute of Certified Public Accountants (AICPA) followed with an In-Process Research and Development (IPR&D) Practice Aid (December 2001) that contained some detailed descriptions of acceptable valuation premises and practices. In January 2003, AICPA issued Statement on Auditing Standards (SAS) 101, which established the auditor's role in assessing fair value measurement; finally, in June 2006, SFAS 157, *Fair Value Measurements*, was issued; a final revised version as Accounting Standards Codification (ASC) 820 followed on May 12, 2011.

The term *fair value* has always related to financial reporting, whereas *fair market value* in the United States and Canada, plus *market value* in much of the rest of the world, is now usually linked to tax reporting and financing requirements. But fair value has always been stated to be market-based, and many practitioners have considered it to be synonymous with fair market value. This is changing. FASB has observed that the U.S. definition of fair market value, which is, in effect, set out in U.S. Revenue Ruling 54-60, relates principally to assets (property) and has attached to it a significant legal content. Because such interpretive case law may not be relevant for financial reporting, FASB chose to develop its own definition (described in Chapter 2) that is free of past interpretations and case law and represents an "exit" price based on the new concept of market participants rather than willing buyers and willing sellers.

Under both IFRS and GAAP, there is a major distinction between the two terms: Fair value does not consider the point of view of a willing seller, but is solely an exit price. In Chapter 4 a simplified example shows that fair value using market participant assumptions can be significantly lower (or possibly higher) than fair market value based on management's expectations.

Fair Value Accounting

The worldwide debate about the role of fair value (as defined in ASC 820) in financial reporting was still under way in 2011. The current model is mixed—some assets, both financial and physical, are carried at amortized cost, most of the rest at fair values. However, disclosures in both the financial statements and their notes provide additional fair value information for both groups. Most practitioners agree that the present situation creates anomalies and challenges. There is no potential consensus, as there are a number of arguments for and against the complete adoption of fair value accounting. They are grouped into objective and subjective categories in Tables 1.1 and 1.2.

TABLE 1.1 Objective Arguments Supporting and Opposing Fair Value Accounting

Supporting	Opposing
Easy to explain	Sometimes difficult and costly to determine and audit
Always relevant	More susceptible to bias when estimated
Prevents some transaction structuring	May create inconsistency due to different models and inputs
Promotes consistency	Not always useful, such as factories versus financial instruments
Provides basis for investment decision	
Improves transparency	Could be confusing when combined with transaction flows in income statement
	Lacks relevance when assets are to be held

TABLE 1.2 Subjective Arguments For and Against Fair Value

Supporting	Opposing
It ensures correct timing of impairment losses.	In some cases, there is no real market, only a notional one.
It is a useful early indicator of problems.	Markets can be wrong; management's estimates of future cash flows may be better.
Management intent may produce harmful bias.	Market pessimism or optimism is irrelevant if there is no intent or need to sell.
Losses cannot be masked.	Too much information exacerbates market spikes, as undue pessimism and irrational fear may create downward spirals; the inverse is also true.

INVESTMENT BANKERS VERSUS VALUATORS

Of the professionals involved in preparing valuations, investment bankers and valuators are the most important. As an aside, I have been both; the former in my twenties when I could easily pull an all-nighter for a bulge bracket (top-level) Wall Street firm, then the latter for most of the past 40 years. Both are heavily involved in determining values but for very different purposes. Ideally, they should work together for the benefit of their mutual client.

Typically, the investment banker brings two parties, the potential buyer and the reluctant seller, together and assists them in finding a sufficiently mutually beneficial price that makes a deal possible. This is important to that professional, as much of the investment bank's revenue is performance based. In the process, there is always some valuation activity, often a considerable amount. If the deal involves a public offering or a private placement of securities, there may be regulatory requirements for an independent valuation. As well, there is frequently the need or desire, by one party or the other, to obtain independent information on the soundness and future financial and economic viability of the transaction and the entities resulting from its completion, as well as its fairness to both parties.

Following closing, the valuator comes into his or her own, as independence is essential for the PPA process that has to be undertaken at fair values. In addition, normally there are compliance issues and requirements for financial, tax, and often statutory filings. Whether the work is done by a valuator, by an investment banker, or internally, the need to know the value of a business has global application, especially today with joint ventures, domestic consolidations, public listings, and increased foreign investment.

 ## VALUATION REQUIREMENTS

Valuation involves some qualitative but mainly quantitative activities. Neither totally an art nor completely alchemy, it is a hybrid, driven by judgments that consider universal, basic economic principles, such as supply, scarcity, demand, substitution, and utility. There are three generally adopted approaches: market, cost (asset-based), and income. These are discussed in more detail in Chapters 6, 7, and 8, respectively.

In the larger picture, a business is usually thought of as a combination of resources (financial, physical, intangible, and human) that absorb inputs and generate outputs, rather than just a summation of the underlying assets. The

TABLE 1.3 Needs of Financial Statement Users

User	Need
Auditors	Asset values
Bankruptcy judges	Both business and asset values
Board of directors	Equity values
Financial analysts	Both business and asset values
Investment bankers	Aggregate business value
Legal counsel	Both business and asset values
Management	Usually both, as compensation may be tied to returns
Regulators	Both business and asset values
Shareholders	Equity values
Tax authorities	Asset values

invested capital (the sum of debt and equity) represents the total enterprise value (TEV) of the business; this must obviously equal the total of the fair values of each of the assets, liabilities, and equity.

A business valuation usually assesses the underlying earnings and cash flows generated by the resources involved and does not place a particular amount on each individual item. Asset appraisers, sometimes the same individuals but wearing another hat, look mainly at specific items and do not spend much time on the entire entity's economic position. There are strong demands for both, as shown in Table 1.3, which sets out the needs of 10 typical types of users.

LITIGATION RISKS

Finally, we must deal with a significant but not often discussed problem: securities (shareholder) litigation, which cost U.S. enterprises more than $35 billion in settlements from 1996 to 2005. Often, when investors lose money, they feel the loss was not due to their bad decisions, but was somebody else's fault, so their first thought is "Who can I sue?" The introduction of fair value reporting is likely to result in increased litigation, especially in the United States, but also in other countries. This is because estimating fair value is based on principles, not rules, and therefore requires significant judgment. In hindsight, it is sometimes easy for litigants to question any of the judgments exercised by valuators, financial statements preparers, or those auditing them.

Certainly not a lot of judgment is required for a valuation using Level 1 inputs of the three-level fair value hierarchy (discussed in Chapter 3); the market price for an identical asset is what it is. There are more judgments in valuations using Level 2 inputs of adjusted data, or information from analogous markets. For example, a plaintiff's lawyer might ask a valuator, "How did you make the decision that market A was similar enough to market B that its prices are satisfactory Level 2 inputs for items traded in market B?" For Level 3 inputs (everything else), there are considerably more judgments involved, especially in preparing financial projections (discussed in Chapter 5), as well as using them in Discounted Cash Flow (DCF) valuation models (Chapter 8).

Undoubtedly plaintiffs will aggressively try to second-guess most judgments. A basic allegation is likely to be that an impairment write-down should have been made earlier than it was. In a Level 3 case, they will say that the models were based on improper assumptions, the projections were poorly constructed, and so on. This focus, of attacking well-supported judgments based on subsequent happenings, will be heightened in the United States if there is a move toward IFRS with its principles-based accounting, which requires more judgments, and away from GAAP's rules-based accounting, which involves far fewer.

Such attacks will begin in the early stages of the litigation, due to the 2007 *Tellabs* decision by the U.S. Supreme Court. That body held that, before a securities matter can even get to the discovery stage, a court must weigh the allegations in the complaint and decide if they suggest fraud or its absence. Where the suggestion of fraud is at least as strong as its absence, the case goes forward; otherwise it does not.

What this means, in fair value–related securities lawsuits, is that a court at the outset will be called upon to consider whether the accounting and valuation judgments that were made, in connection with whatever procedure is being challenged, are tainted by fraud or they appear to have been made in good faith. This focus isn't necessarily a bad thing for defendants. Describing how well-supported judgments, exercised in good faith, were undertaken can be a very effective defense with judges, but not necessarily with juries, whose eyes may glaze over from hearing the details. While it may be an excellent defense, the questioning of many accounting and valuation judgments in cross-examination is undoubtedly going to increase legal and other costs and give rise to anxieties among valuators.

TEN COMMANDMENTS OF VALUATION

To end this chapter, I have appended my 10 commandments of valuation. The Bible expresses the original commandments as "Thou shalt not . . ."; I prefer to express mine as "Thou shalt . . ."

1. *Look to the long term.* The stock market is oriented to short-term returns, but it is far easier to anticipate longer-term trends than to guess what will happen next week. Nobody can tell what the price of oil is going to be in three months, although speculators constantly bet on it, but nearly everyone can be certain that in five years it will be significantly higher than it is now. For example, when adjusting for lack of marketability, consider how long of a holding period may be involved.

2. *Hunt for information.* Start with the readily available information that every buyer or seller knows as well as you do. Then undertake wide-ranging due diligence, evaluating customers as well as competitors, their managements, and their markets. Many managers are unaware of all their existing and potential competitors. There are roughly 20,000 entities with traded securities in North America, and over 40,000 worldwide. Screen just about every one of them to find those similar to the subject; also look at databases such as Dun & Bradstreet or Hoover's for information on private competitors.

3. *Be skeptical of sources.* Always check the facts and strive to understand the biases and potential conflicts of interest in every source; make sure that the raw data gives suitable information for the intended purposes.

4. *Strive for effective rationality.* It is vital to sort the available information and grade it for quality, so as to filter out the inevitable noise.

5. *Be understanding.* In developing a capitalization rate, don't just rely on taking data from a respected source such as Ibbotson or Duff & Phelps. Seek out the real risks and potential returns of the business and quantify them to generate a rate for the entity commensurate with reported acquisition multiples.

6. *Stay humble.* Hubris leads to failure, while humility breeds an open mind that continually seeks good information and is willing to heed advice.

7. *Know your limits.* Unless you are prepared to do a lot of industry homework and you have a knowledgeable mentor, don't take on a job in a field you don't understand.

8. *Stay in your circle of competence.* This is complementary to "know your limits." Remaining in familiar countries or industries you know is the best way to be consistently sure-footed.

9. *Be a contrarian.* Existing trends won't continue forever—they never have. Bull or bear, markets can take a long time to develop. If you sense a distant upward or downward trend in an industry or sector, build it into your projections in two or so years, even if your peers look askance.

10. *Be adaptable.* Look at all possible valuation techniques; what works well at one time may be useless at another.

CHAPTER TWO

Fair Value Concept

All values are anticipations of the future.

—Oliver Wendell Holmes (1841–1935), American jurist

C HAPTER 1 DEALT WITH THE SIGNIFICANCE OF VALUE. Now we turn to fair value as a concept; this is followed in Chapter 3 by a discussion of the framework used to determine the appropriate amount. While fair market value or market value has been used in tax codes of many nations for more than a century, fair value is still very new; in 1979, the Financial Accounting Standards Board (FASB) issued Statement of Financial Accounting Standards (SFAS) 33, *Financial Reporting and Changing Prices*, which required firms to disclose in the notes to their financial statements current cost information, which in effect reflected market values. In the United States, fair value became fully developed with a common definition for all users in 2006 on the issuance of the SFAS 157. In May 2011, with minor improvements, as Accounting Standards Codification (ASC) 820, it was fully converged with International Financial Reporting Standards (IFRS) 13, integrating the notion in just about every country around the world and making financial statements more significant worldwide.

RELEVANT PRONOUNCEMENTS

Over 60 Generally Accepted Accounting Principles (GAAP) in the United States and IFRS pronouncements incorporate fair value in some manner. The main assets, liabilities, or transactions whose accounting treatment is affected include:

- Debt and equity securities
- Almost all assets acquired and liabilities assumed in a business combination
- Guarantee liabilities
- Nonmonetary transactions
- Contributions of services
- Derivatives
- Asset retirement obligations
- Impairments of a single or group of long-lived assets
- Restructuring liabilities

 DEFINITIONS

While many readers may consider the subject complicated, when applying fair value it is crucial to understand its definition and how it differs from other measures. ASC 820 defines it as:

> The price that would be received to sell an asset or paid to transfer a liability in an orderly transaction between market participants at the measurement date.

This is an exit price as it relates to "the price that would be received" and therefore is not the same as the well-established fair market value (United States and Canada) and market value (rest of the world).

Fair market value is a tax construct where the adjective *fair* relates to the noun *market* rather than to *value*. It is defined in the United States according to the *International Glossary of Business Valuation Terms* (International Glossary) as:

> The price at which the property would change hands between a willing buyer and a willing seller when the former is not under any compulsion to buy and the latter is not under any compulsion to sell, both parties having reasonable knowledge of relevant facts, are able, as well as willing, to trade and are well-informed about the property and the market for such property.

In Canada the word *highest* is inserted before the term *price*.

Those definitions are subject to well-developed bodies of rules, regulations, judicial decisions, and commentaries. They are intended to represent the activities of hypothetical conventional buyers and sellers and, as such, to reflect a consensus price of a transaction for the asset or security after it has been exposed to a broad market for a reasonable period. All generally accepted valuation methods were developed to establish fair market value and have been adapted to determine fair values.

The definition for market value from the International Valuation Standards is very similar to that of fair market value:

> The estimated amount for which a property should exchange on the date of valuation between a willing buyer and a willing seller in an arm's-length transaction after proper marketing wherein the parties had each acted knowledgably, prudently, and without compulsion.

In each case the resulting number is a midpoint or entry price, rather than an exit price. It is important to note that the current definition of fair value introduced the key feature of market participants. This is intended to ensure that its measurements are market-based rather than entity-specific, which fair market value or market value often is. All these versions of value reflect economic truth plus measurement errors and management biases.

MARKET PARTICIPANTS

Market participants, a key feature of fair value, are industrial or financial organizations that buy and sell in the particular market involved. They are similar to, but not the same as, the willing buyers and willing sellers referred to in the definitions of both fair market value and market value. A market participant must be:

- Independent of the relevant entity
- Knowledgeable about the item and potential sale from available information, including usual and customary due diligence efforts
- Financially able to enter into a hypothetical transaction for the item
- Willing, motivated, but not forced or otherwise compelled to deal

Depending on the item, the range of market participants will vary widely, including both industrial and financial buyers. For a vacant manufacturing facility they would include speculators as well as potential users, while for a reporting unit (under GAAP) or cash-generating unit (under IFRS; see Chapter 14) they could comprise a wide variety of venture capital firms as well as known or potential competitors.

In identifying candidates, management should consider factors specific to the asset, the market, and entities to which they might sell. A potential profile must be prepared, but participants need not be identified. In most cases, the process is straightforward, as management will have a general knowledge of probable buyers. Sometimes it is necessary to make assumptions about others that might be interested.

When there is no apparent exit market, as is the case for many intangible assets, an entity should establish the characteristics of market participants (both industrial and financial) to which it could theoretically sell the item. Once those are determined, their assumptions as to how to price it should be identified. This may best be done by constructing a hypothetical market for the asset, based on management's views about what others would take into account in negotiating a purchase. Likely considerations include the asset's specific location, condition, assumed market growth, expected depreciation, availability of synergies, and appropriate risk premiums.

 ## FAIR VALUE ACCOUNTING

There are many active and inactive markets, broadly defined, for financial instruments and many other assets. Information acquisition costs are falling partly due to the Internet making more market data immediately available, while estimating fair values is easier due to more and better statistical models. This has led to increased demand from investors and other users for expanded fair value accounting. However, there is substantial push-back from managements due to the difficulties in implementation and the resulting volatility in net income. The question therefore is not whether accounting should be predominantly based on amortized historical costs or fair values, but how, in a mixed attribute model, an asset, liability, or equity should be recorded.

 ## REVALUATION UNDER IFRS

Under IAS 16, *Property, Plant & Equipment*, and IAS 40, *Investment Properties*, entities may choose to record selected physical assets using either the historical cost or the revaluation model. Under the latter:

- Assets are shown at fair values on the balance sheet.
- Changes in fair values go to a revaluation reserve.
- Impairment is charged first to the revaluation reserve.
- Such charges may be reversed if circumstances change.
- Value in use (to the firm rather than market participants) is allowed for.
- Net income volatility is lower than under full fair value accounting.

OTHER TYPES OF VALUE

Professionals need to be aware of other categories of value that are mentioned in this book.

Legal Fair Value

Just to confuse things, a number of jurisdictions, mainly in the United States, use the term *fair value* in statutes relating to divorce or shareholder disputes. While specific interpretations differ by area, the term's ancestry dates back to the early nineteenth century. According to the Principles of Corporate Governance issued by the American Law Institute, this fair value is defined as:

> The value of the eligible holder's proportionate interest in the corporation, without any discount for minority status or . . . lack or marketability . . . using customary valuation concepts and techniques.

This is the opposite of fair value, which allows appropriate discounts for both absence of control (DAOC) and lack of marketability (DLOM).

Liquidation Value

Under certain circumstances, such as the failure of a business or to establish collateral for a loan, a liquidation value may be needed. This differs from fair value because it normally involves a compulsion to sell. In liquidations, assets are generally disposed of on a piecemeal basis, not as a going concern.

There are two kinds of liquidation—orderly and forced. An orderly liquidation assumes the assets will be sold over a period long enough to permit normal exposure in an appropriate secondary market. In U.S. bankruptcies, a period of up to 18 months has been allowed in establishing orderly liquidation values. Forced liquidation is based on a lower level of exposure over a shorter period and is sometimes referred to as auction value.

Orderly liquidation value has not been judicially defined, but for assets, the traditional view may be paraphrased as:

> The most likely price, expressed in terms of money, realizable in a market in which similar property is regularly sold to willing buyers. The seller is compelled to sell, but in an orderly and advertised manner over a reasonable period on an "as is, where is" basis, with the buyer being responsible for removal costs.

For an entity, the comparable definition would be:

> The net amount expected to be realized if the business is terminated, the assets sold on an orderly basis, and the creditors paid off as part of the closing. The net amount is after expenses connected with liquidation, such as legal, accounting, and certain holding and disposal costs.

When accounting for discontinued operations or assets that are to be sold, this definition should be considered. In such an event, any expenses connected to the sale, including marketing and disposal costs, are deducted.

Intrinsic Value

The term *intrinsic value* is applied to a generalized version of fair value. According to Investopedia, it relates the "actual" value of a company or asset based on an underlying perception of its true value including all aspects of the business in terms of both tangible and intangible factors. Normally, as it is based on a broad range of so-called trade buyers, rather than market participants or even one particular prospective owner, it may include entity-specific assumptions. It is the measure commonly used by financial analysts to establish price targets for stocks they consider undervalued or, less frequently, overvalued.

Investment Value

According the International Glossary, the investment value of an asset is:

> The value to a particular owner based on individual investment requirements and expectations.

This amount is subjective, and as such, it differs in nature from the other concepts of value that are intended to be objective, impersonal, and detached. It is the maximum amount a particular prospective owner would pay, particularly for intangible assets. The most important use of investment value is in helping managements avoid overpaying in merger and acquisition transactions.

Strategic buyers are frequently prepared to offer a substantially greater amount than the market participants (often financial buyers) who establish fair value. This is due to available synergies (the results of cooperation and combinations with existing activities or situations that increase the effectiveness or efficiency of one or more of the acquired elements), improved market access, and other expected advantages. For investment value, the willing buyer is not a participant in a notional (hypothetical) market, but a special purchaser with specific expectations about future events. As a result of these factors, a strategic buyer paying investment value may achieve a similar return, with comparable or lower risks, than market participants paying the lesser amount of fair value, as the latter establish their purchase prices solely on expected returns and probable risks.

 ## VALUATION PRINCIPLES

Three key principles are always applicable when measuring the fair values of either individual assets or securities that represent a group of assets and liabilities:

1. *Alternatives.* In any transaction, each party has alternatives to closing the deal.
2. *Substitution.* The maximum amount a prudent buyer will pay for an asset or security is the cost to construct or develop an item of equal functionality (effectiveness) and utility (efficiency), allowing for time to market.
3. *Future benefits.* Another measure of the ceiling a buyer will pay for an asset or security is the present value of the future benefits expected by its owner.

Six secondary factors are also important:

1. *Supply and demand:* Fluctuations in supply of, or demand for, the output of an asset or an entity may cause both costs and benefits to vary, as can the availability of alternatives
2. *External factors:* Alterations in the situation in which it operates may cause an asset or business to be worth more or less than historical cost
3. *Functional deterioration:* This occurs when an asset or business is no longer able to perform its functions or offer the utility for which it was designed or acquired

4. *Physical decline:* The reduction in functionality or utility of an asset due to age or use
5. *Technological obsolescence:* Reduction in productive abilities of an asset resulting from lack of improvement in design, engineering, or technology
6. *Economic deprivation:* A decrease in the value of an asset or entity due to changes in the economic situation beyond the owner's control rather than because of its current use or condition

The impact of the last four secondary factors is not the same as the financial term commonly called depreciation, which amortizes the cost of an asset against income over its estimated useful life.

 ## REPORTING AND CASH-GENERATING UNITS

Reporting units and cash-generating units are important terms, discussed in detail in Chapter 14. For impairment testing purposes, all assets and liabilities of an entity have to be allocated to either a reporting unit (GAAP) or a cash-generating unit (IFRS). Therefore, management, auditors, and valuators all need to agree on how many relevant units there are within an entity and which of them have goodwill.

A reporting unit is defined as an operating segment or a first-level component of one. An operating segment is an element of an entity that earns revenue and incurs expenses for which discrete financial information is available. Management, in the form of a "chief operating decision maker," should regularly review the operating results of each component to determine the allocation of the firm's resources. Generally, reporting units have local managers who maintain contact with the chief operating decision maker to discuss operating activities, financial results, and future plans. Many companies decide to have only one reporting unit if possible. The advantage is that the goodwill from one acquisition that might be impaired may be covered by a better-performing activity.

A cash-generating unit is the smallest identifiable group of assets that generates cash inflows that are largely independent of those from other assets or groups of assets. The difference from a reporting unit may be demonstrated by the example of a small (six-unit) retail chain. This would be a single reporting unit but seven cash-generating units: one for each of the stores, as they generate cash independently, and a final one for the central warehouse that holds the chain's inventory.

CHAPTER THREE

Fair Value Framework

Get a good idea and stay with it. Work at it until
it's done and done right.

—*Walt Disney (1901–1960), American showman*

T HE PREVIOUS CHAPTER DISCUSSED the concept of fair value;
this one deals with calculating the amount. Then we go on to the more
interesting topics of "Taming the Future" (Chapter 4) and "Projecting
What Is to Come" (Chapter 5). The two converged standards, ASC 820 and
IFRS 13, define an exit price and create an underlying conceptual framework
for establishing the necessary amounts. This has six stages:

1. Determine the unit of account.
2. Evaluate the premise of value.
3. Assess the principal market.
4. Establish the most advantageous market.
5. Select appropriate valuation methods.
6. Estimate fair value conclusions.

STAGE 1: DETERMINE THE UNIT OF ACCOUNT

The first stage in arriving at the fair value of an asset, security, technology, liability, or business interest is to clearly identify exactly what is to be valued; this is known as the *unit of account*. It may be a single asset (a stand-alone office building), a liability or security, a group of related assets (a functioning machine shop), a reporting or cash-generating unit, an ownership interest in an entity, or even a complete enterprise.

It is based on the level at which the accounting for the item takes place and the extent it is required to be aggregated or disaggregated in accordance with any applicable GAAP or IFRS rules. For example:

▪ Depreciation is usually calculated for individual operating assets.
▪ An allowance for doubtful accounts may be determined by individual customers or for pools of similar purchasers.
▪ Goodwill impairment is measured for each reporting unit or cash-generating unit.

In some cases the relevant standard defines the unit of account; in others judgment is needed to determine the appropriate quantity. If the authoritative literature requires valuing a single item (such as a traded share), then that is the unit of account; if it refers to valuing a group of assets (for instance a fleet of the same model trucks), then the group is the unit of account.

As subsequently discussed, the fair values of all physical and intangible assets have to be based on their highest and best use; in 2011 this was prohibited for financial assets. For a piece of real estate, the unit of account is usually the single asset, even if the amount has to be disaggregated for reporting purposes. Under GAAP, this is separated into at least land and building. For IFRS, it will be land, structure, and appropriate elements, such as heating, ventilation, and air-conditioning (HVAC) and electrical systems; under that regime each part of property, plant & equipment (PP&E) with "a cost that is significant in relation to the whole" has to be depreciated separately over its useful life. Therefore, after a physical asset's fair value is obtained, by, say, the market approach, it often has to be broken down into individual accounting elements, normally by the cost approach.

Examples of a unit of account are:

▪ A loan portfolio (financial asset)
▪ An individual loan (financial asset)

- A single publicly traded security (financial asset)
- All the interests in a privately owned entity (financial asset)
- An office building (physical asset)
- An operating plant (physical asset)
- A brand (intangible asset)

All specific characteristics of the asset must be reflected; the most important are:

- *Condition.* Relatively new and very old items should not be combined.
- *Location.* Equipment such as automobiles at various sites should be treated individually, as such markets vary from location to location.
- *Restrictions on sale or use.* Freely tradable securities are different from restricted ones.

Value the Actual Assets

It is essential that the items being valued are reconciled to the assets and liabilities reported on the related financial statements. This is to make sure that everything that has been recorded is included. It is also necessary to verify that they are actually the same, not merely similar. Problems arise if proper records have not been maintained and the balance sheet does not agree with reality. Often valuators must use what they find in the field and, after preparing a complete listing of all the existing assets, adjust the financial statements accordingly.

Another difficult situation is to determine the fair value of the intangibles that arise from day-to-day relationships with customers or suppliers, or those directly connected to a financial or physical asset. For example, a purchaser of a bank branch with deposits and loans, credit card portfolios, or insurance liabilities often accepts a lower-than-market yield by paying a premium for possible future business or cross-selling opportunities. The only items recognized on the financial statements as assets or liabilities are those that represent existing balances that can be transferred as financial items; the associated customer relationships are a separate intangible. This is to prevent a fair value measurement from becoming a device for recognizing internally developed intangibles.

When creating the relevant assets, however, the seller has incurred costs to secure the customer relationships, although they were likely expensed at the time. A buyer purchases not only the financial and physical assets, but also the related intangible; the observed or notional market premium (say 14% of book value) is simply a means of measuring them. The interaction between fair value and unrecognized, internally created intangibles remains a complex unresolved issue.

Example

The following example is based on *Understanding the Issues*, Volume 3, Series 1, by John M. Foster, a FASB member at the time, and Wayne S. Upton, then a senior FASB project manager and now Director, International Activities at IASB. It highlights the need to carefully define an item before estimating its fair value.

A riverfront property is operated as a marina. The present value of its cash flows is $500,000. Based on recent sales of adjacent properties, the land alone has a value of $700,000. That amount is the fair value of the PP&E on the financial statements. This is a component of the marina operation, the value of which includes both the physical assets and unrecorded intangibles. As the "lowest level for which there are identifiable cash flows that are largely independent" is the marina as a whole, there is no way to separate the business cash flows from those of the land.

There are at least two possible reasons why the present value of the cash flows from operations is below the current market value of the land. The first is that management correctly estimated the cash flows associated with the marina, but assigned a low terminal value to the land and used a discount rate higher than that acceptable to land buyers. This seems unlikely, especially as the land will become more valuable once some recently sold adjacent properties are developed. Therefore, the second possibility is more probable; the marina will incur extra costs, with a present value of $200,000 over its remaining life, reflecting cleanup of the site, demolition of the existing buildings, taxes, and so on.

In either case, the fair value of the PP&E shown on the balance sheet is $700,000. The difference from the $500,000 present value of the cash flows reflects future operating costs that neither meet the definition of a liability nor affect the value of the asset. ■

STAGE 2: EVALUATE THE PREMISE OF VALUE

The next stage is evaluating the premise of value to be applied under the overall conceptual framework. There are two basic premises: value in combination with other assets or stand-alone value; the amount measured under one premise will differ from that of the same item under the other.

In Combination

Value in combination is based on an asset's highest and best use being its ability, jointly with other assets and liabilities, to contribute to a going concern. The concept normally relates to an entity, business enterprise, reporting unit, or cash-generating unit and assumes that it is conducting ordinary operations. It also applies to assets involved in generating income, assuming that they are configured for the purpose and currently in active use for that function.

Stand-Alone

The concept of stand-alone value is based on a separate sale; it compares the asset to the situation of comparable items available in the market.

Highest and Best Use

The premise selected is established based on the highest and best use of the asset by market participants, which may differ from management's intended application. For example, an entity operates and plans to continue to operate a property as a restaurant, yet, if market participants consider the highest and best use is as a parking lot, the latter would establish fair value.

The concept of highest and best use, which relates only to physical and intangible assets, refers to use that provides maximum value to market participants and is legally allowable, physically possible, and financially feasible. The legally allowable criterion mainly applies to real estate; the physically possible criterion, which applies to both real estate and operating activities, relates to such items as the availability of water, gas, and electricity; while the financially feasible criterion refers to the expected return on the proposed use.

Offsetting Credit Risks

The removal of the in-use premise for financial assets has created problems in valuing such items and related liabilities when they are managed together as portfolios. The converged standards of May 2011 include specific guidance for financial assets and liabilities with offsetting market or counterparty credit risks. This will permit measuring their fair values using prices for the net position; it will also apply to any derivatives, which may not be considered financial assets or liabilities.

For example, entities can apply this guidance when an interest rate risk is being managed by the group of assets and liabilities, but not when the group is used to manage all market risks; it may be used only when:

- The entity manages the group on the basis of the net exposure to particular risks based on documented strategies.
- Management is given information on the basis of net risk exposures.
- The net exposures to particular risks are managed consistently.
- The assets and liabilities within the group are reported at fair values in the statement of financial position.

When those criteria are met, the standards require entities to measure the fair value of the group by applying the price within the bid-ask spread that is most representative for the overall portfolio under the circumstances. If there is a legally enforceable right to offset assets and liabilities on a counterparty's default (e.g., a netting agreement), adjustments are made to the net exposure to reflect the counterparty's credit risk.

Although in limited circumstances the standards permit valuing groups of financial instruments, the unit of account remains the individual item. Existing pronouncement requirements continue; therefore netting offsetting positions is permitted only when the existing criteria are met. Values based on net risk exposure will be prohibited for financial assets and liabilities with available Level 1 inputs (see "Fair Value Hierarchy" subsection in Stage 5).

Blockage Factors

Often, such as for many financial assets or some physical ones, quoted prices for an identical item in an active market are available; those are classified as Level 1 inputs in the fair value hierarchy. In such cases the relevant fair value must be determined by multiplying the quantity held by the quoted price. GAAP and IFRS preclude adjustments (blockage factors) to quoted prices to reflect the size of the position relative to normal trading, even if such adjustments frequently occur in practice. However, the standards permit control premiums and discounts for absence of control or lack of marketability when market participants would consider them.

Shareholders' Equity

Until 2011 GAAP and IFRS did not contain guidance on valuing an entity's own shares held in shareholders' equity. The converged standards require such fair values to represent exit prices from the perspective of market participants, who would hold the shares as assets.

Restricted Assets

Certain items have restrictions on sale or transferability. Their fair value should reflect the discount, if any, that market participants in general would require as a result.

Example

Land is donated to a not-for-profit organization subject to contractual restrictions on its use. If the limitations were not legally transferred on a sale, they are specific to the organization and other owners could use the land however they wished, subject to its existing zoning. As the restrictions would be disregarded by market participants, they do not affect fair value. If they would be legally transferred, then an appropriate discount, probably substantial, must be applied. ▓

Defensive Assets

A defensive asset is an acquired asset, usually an intangible, that an entity does not plan to actively use, but intends to hold (lock up) to prevent others from obtaining access to it. An example is a trade name acquired in a business combination that the buyer does not intend to use or sell. It does not plan to use the name, because it wishes to expand its own existing brand, and it does not propose to sell it, as it wants to avoid a competitor having access to it.

Before ASC 820, most valuators believed that the buyer's objective should be taken into consideration when estimating such fair values. Because the buyer intended to put a defensive asset on a shelf and not use it, some considered that it must not have any value, ascribing only a nominal amount to its fair value. The converged standards clearly state that a market participant's perspective, based on the highest and best use, should be used when estimating the fair value of every asset. The highest and best use to a market participant would likely be to use the name rather than put it on a shelf; however, even if this was so, its fair value would not be nominal, as there is some benefit in not allowing others to use it.

Interaction of Unit of Account and Valuation Premises

Even when the in-combination premise is applicable, the fair value of an asset is still a market-oriented measurement based on how it would be used by market participants, which should reflect all specific facts and circumstances. The in-combination premise may even apply to a single unit of account, such as a reporting or cash-generating unit, if the underlying assets are used together. It also applies when combining multiple units. Once the exit market has been determined, market participants' assumptions for each valuation premise are developed based on iterative interactions between it and conditions in the selected market.

The unit of account represents the item being valued. GAAP and IFRS both specify that the appropriate unit is that which is "expected to yield the most advantageous exchange price" in a reference market to which the entity has reasonable access. Therefore individual units should be aggregated to achieve their highest and best use from the perspective of market participants and to reflect the entity's access to the relevant market. A single unit of account may be included in only one grouping. In establishing the appropriate market, management should consider which combinations would provide the highest value. The notion of "the most advantageous exchange price" presumes rational market behavior and a single agreed-upon market-clearing price resulting from the interaction of market participants as willing buyers and sellers. The choice of the reference market is covered in Stages 3 and 4.

Disaggregation determines the fair value of a unit of account based on individual sales of its components; this applies if such sales would maximize the amount and the entity has access to the relevant markets. However, caution should be exercised in estimating fair values on this basis. Only when there is strong evidence that market participants would disaggregate to maximize their return may this be regarded as the highest and best use. If an asset such as an automobile is customarily sold at a level below the full unit of account (the firm's fleet at a single location), an entity may consider the markets into which the components could be sold as indications of fair value. Each asset must be valued in its current form, and the costs of any transformation or value-adding activity, such as renovation or replacing parts, must be subtracted. When applying the concepts of both aggregation and disaggregation, it is critical to ensure that the ultimate value relates solely to the unit of account and not, even in part, to any additions.

Establishing the highest and best use of an asset is an integral part of identifying potential markets where it can be sold, and determines the appropriate valuation premise either in combination or stand-alone.

Example: Unit of Account Individual Mortgages

Mutual Bank is estimating the fair value of the various loans in its mortgage portfolio. It has access to markets for both individual mortgages and securitized loans. Historically, the bank has sold a majority of its mortgages through securitizations. Management determines that the sale of individual mortgages (mainly to groups of investors) is not its principal market. A portfolio of individual mortgages is often aggregated and transformed into securities through a sale to a trust, which undertakes a subsequent distribution, by a prospectus, of beneficial interests to investors. Those securities are usually arranged in *tranches*, which add additional security to the senior level. A bank with access to the securitization market should consider it in establishing the most advantageous market for its individual mortgages.

However, securitization involves costs, and an estimate of their impact must be subtracted to obtain the amount attributed to the unit of account (the individual mortgage), as fair value relates to the actual asset involved and not what it may become. Depending on the facts and circumstances, it is often reasonable to incorporate assumptions relating to planned activities and their costs; this allows estimation of a market price by working backward from an expected outcome. ▪

STAGE 3: ASSESS THE PRINCIPAL MARKET

The definition of fair value assumes that the transaction occurs in the principal market for the asset or liability, or in its absence, the most advantageous market, defined from the standpoint of the entity. The principal market is that in which it conducts its highest volume or level of activity. Without evidence to the contrary, the market in which an entity would normally enter into a transaction is assumed to be the principal market. If there is not one, the most advantageous must be found. Different entities in the same enterprise group may have separate principal markets for identical assets or liabilities, depending on their activities, where they are located, and which they can access. Restrictions on the transfer of an asset or a liability are not considered in determining the principal market.

There are several types of markets to be taken into account. In assessing whether a valuation input is observable, management should consider the characteristics of the market involved:

- *Exchange markets.* Closing prices from actual trades are both readily available and representative of fair value.
- *Dealer markets.* Firms stand ready to trade for their own accounts, thereby providing liquidity, by holding an inventory of the relevant items. Typically, bid and ask prices are more readily available than closing prices; such markets are common for financial instruments, commodities, materials, and selected capital assets (automobiles and some equipment).
- *Broker markets.* Participants actively match buyers with sellers but do not stand ready to trade for their own accounts; the most common example is real estate. For a broker quote to be observable, an entity needs knowledge of the market data used to develop it.
- *Principal markets.* Transactions (both originations and resales) are negotiated independently by buyers and sellers, with no intermediaries. Very little information about these dealings is usually available.

If the entity has a principal market for a particular asset, it can expedite Stages 3 and 4. Otherwise, after determining potential markets, their participants, and valuation premises, management must establish which are accessible by reviewing the appropriate indicators of value. Determining the fair value of an asset may involve estimating the amount it could be sold for in more than one potential market to which the owner has access, as well as examining both the in-combination and stand-alone exchange premises.

If an entity regularly buys or sells a particular asset in a single market, that is its principal market; if it deals in several, the appropriate one is that which represents a majority of its volumes. In most cases, the principal market is also the most advantageous. Management does not have to continuously evaluate multiple prices for an asset to determine the most advantageous market, but it cannot incorporate potentially more advantageous markets into fair value measurements when it has a principal market.

STAGE 4: ESTABLISH THE MOST ADVANTAGEOUS MARKET

If the entity does not have a principal market for a particular asset, it should evaluate all accessible potential markets, based on the highest and best use from the perspective of their participants, to establish the most advantageous. Often, there is more than one potential exit market, multiple possible uses, and many participants. However, managements are not required to search all potential markets for the most advantageous price, nor do they have to undertake all possible efforts to obtain data concerning the assumptions that market participants would adopt. They need only apply reasonably available information to develop a profile of market participants.

When assessing the valuation premise, management should consider realistic scenarios as to how identified market participants would use the asset, based on its nature, history, knowledge of the market, and other relevant information. After an entity has determined potential markets, it roughly values the asset in each of them. The most advantageous is the one that, after transaction costs, results in the highest receipt for an asset or the lowest payment to transfer a liability.

Orderly Transactions

An orderly transaction assumes exposure to the market for a period prior to the measurement date to allow for marketing activities that are usual and customary for transactions involving such assets or liabilities. It is also one that has not been coerced; a distressed sale is not an orderly transaction, and neither is a forced liquidation. There are no criteria for how long a deal must be exposed for it to be considered orderly. In general, the longer the period, the more likely it is that the transaction is orderly. However, the nature of the transaction and the market involved must be taken into consideration when determining if the exposure was sufficient. An equity security with a ready market may only need to be exposed for a matter of hours for its sale to be considered orderly. In contrast, a building with unique features such as a cold-storage warehouse may need at least several months to be so regarded.

The fact that a distressed sale is not an orderly transaction does not mean that every transaction in a distressed market is not orderly; whether it is requires judgment and the consideration of all relevant facts and circumstances. In 2008 and 2009, prices in certain markets and trading volumes in many securities fell (or fluctuated) dramatically. In such cases, there was doubt as to whether transactions in those markets were orderly or distressed sales.

In general, a transaction is not orderly if:

- There was insufficient exposure, so that "usual and customary" marketing activities did not take place.
- Only a few market participants were contacted by the seller during the marketing period.
- The seller has filed for bankruptcy, has been placed in receivership, or is close to either.

▪ Regulatory or legal requirements forced the seller into the transaction.
▪ The realized price fell outside the normal range for transactions in the period for the same or similar items.

Every circumstance on the list is not necessary to reach a conclusion that should be based on the weight of the evidence considering "information that is available without undue cost and effort"; a valuator does not have to undertake exhaustive data-gathering efforts. (See Table 3.1.)

It is important to note that the fair value estimation process may need to establish a market risk premium that compensates an investor for the uncertainties inherent in the projected cash flows from the asset or liability; some of that may relate to nonperformance and liquidity. Transaction data may supply information for the appropriate premium.

Market Selection

The principal or most advantageous market is determined from the perspective of the entity to allow for differences among units when there is more than one business. Different reporting or cash-generating units within an entity may deal in different, perhaps geographically separated, markets. Each particular unit must individually consider its principal or most advantageous market, as not all of them have access to the same outlets in which items can be exchanged. Separate markets, with varying participants, may offer different prices for the same item.

Known markets that are inaccessible, such as those in other countries, may be considered in developing the inputs for a hypothetical market, even though they should not be regarded as either principal markets or most advantageous markets. A single entity may have several fair values for identical or similar assets, depending on the nature and location of the units owning them and the markets in which they could be sold. Each unit must consider the facts and

TABLE 3.1 Effects of Conclusions from the Evidence

Conclusion	Impact on Fair Value
Transaction is not orderly.	Little or no consideration should be given to the data.
Transaction is orderly.	The data must be considered; its importance depends on the size of the transaction, how comparable the subject is to the item involved, and how close the sale is to the valuation date.
Evidence is insufficient to decide.	The data should be considered but does not carry as much weight as that for an orderly transaction.

circumstances appropriate to its valuation of an asset and follow the framework regardless of another unit's holdings of identical or similar items.

The price in the relevant market is not adjusted for transaction costs, as they represent incremental expenses specific to the transaction and will differ depending on its nature; they are considered only in selecting the most advantageous market. When location is a characteristic of an asset, such as inventory or pieces of equipment, fair value includes transportation costs, as moving such items to market is part of the sale process.

Example

Ascendo Inc. identified a certain item of production equipment as being impaired. The amount of the charge depends on its fair value. Identical items have been sold in three markets: retail, wholesale, and auction. None is the principal market, because Ascendo does not regularly sell equipment. As there is no principal market, the fair value is based on the most advantageous market; that is the one generating the highest net proceeds.

Market	Retail	Wholesale	Auction
Sale Price	$10,000	$9,700	$9,500
Transportation Costs	(200)	(300)	(150)
Fair Value	$ 9,800	$9,400	$9,350
Transaction Costs	(500)	—	(200)
Net Proceeds	$ 9,300	$9,400	$9,150

As the wholesale market gives the largest net proceeds, it determines fair value to be $9,400, although the retail market results in a higher amount ($9,800) before transaction costs. Even if no legal or contractual impediments restrict access to the market that would pay the highest price for an item, the costs of selling may make it inappropriate as a reference. ■

STAGE 5: SELECT APPROPRIATE VALUATION METHODS

The standards do not prescribe which valuation techniques apply to fair value measurements, nor do they prioritize them, except to prefer actual prices in active markets. Many methods under one of the accepted valuation approaches—market, income, or cost—may be useful; each is dealt with in a subsequent chapter. All should be considered, and those deemed appropriate in the circumstance should be applied. The choice may be affected by the availability of relevant inputs based on market participants' assumptions, as well as their relative reliability.

When reconciling various amounts, one method frequently may provide the best indication of fair value while others are not as suitable due to either limited data or the type of asset. In most circumstances more than one is appropriate, although based on the choice of assumptions, some of the results may not be equally representative of fair value. If multiple techniques are used, management must weigh the results to reach a range of possible conclusions. Fair value will be the most representative point within that band in the specific circumstances.

The techniques adopted for a particular type of asset must be consistently applied. However, it is appropriate to change them or their application if, based on altered facts and circumstances, another better represents fair value. Variations in a particular method's weighting within multiple techniques may be desirable from time to time to reflect current conditions. Other modifications may also be warranted as new markets develop, additional information becomes available, and valuation methods improve. Revised fair values from alterations in the techniques adopted or their application are treated as changes in accounting estimates, affecting current and future reporting periods.

The Market Approach

The market approach, based on the principle of substitution, uses information from transactions in assets and securities similar to the one being valued. This generates market-derived multiples that are applied to the actual asset to determine an indication of value. A method under this approach should regularly be considered in valuing any financial assets, as a market exists for nearly all such items; it is also helpful for most real estate, machinery, and equipment.

A variant of the market approach, often applied to intangible assets, is the relief-from-royalty method. When using this, the valuator implicitly asks management: "If the firm did not own a particular asset advantageous to its business, what percentage of sales would it be willing to pay for the right to use it?" A review of reported transactions in the large, constantly fluid licensing market often provides a reasonable indication of the appropriate level. The method is based on the principle that the value of an asset can be measured by what a firm would have to pay in royalties to license it from a third party, if it were not owned. Databases that gather and organize comparative licensing transactions are an essential tool for valuing intellectual property. In the United States, several organizations provide such information for a fee.

The Cost (Asset-Based) Approach

The cost approach, based on the principle of alternatives, assumes that a desirable alternative to the asset is either an exact duplicate or a replacement offering the same function and utility. The three common types are duplication (reproduction) cost, replacement cost, and creation cost.

This approach is commonly used for capital-intensive entities, or for those that are liquidating. In practice, the cost approach is appropriate for physical assets and for a small number of intangible assets, such as computer software. For such programs it is often possible to establish the time to market or mean time to customer satisfaction, as well as to estimate the costs to duplicate the program. In those instances, a "build or buy" decision can be applied to determine fair value.

The Income Approach

The income approach is based on the principle of future benefits; it is the most commonly used. Market-based valuations are often impractical due to a lack of available information, and cost-based values are frequently inappropriate since economic value is generally independent of any duplication, replacement, or creation costs. Many income-based methods are well accepted, including capitalization of current net income or cash flows and discounting of future cash flows. Some valuators consider the relief-from-royalty method as part of the income approach. All of them seek the same objective: the current value of the benefits (cash flows or earnings) attributable to the ownership of the particular item.

Fair Value Hierarchy

To increase consistency and comparability, the framework established a three-level fair value hierarchy for inputs—the assumptions, risk assessments, and underlying data that market participants use to make pricing decisions. It distinguishes between inputs directly observable in the marketplace (more objective) and those that are unobservable (more subjective):

> *Level 1:* Observable, quoted prices (unadjusted) for identical items in active markets.
> *Level 2:* Quoted prices for similar items in active markets or for identical/similar items in inactive markets, together with the results of pricing models whose inputs are directly or indirectly observable for substantially the full term, or are otherwise derived from observable market data.
> *Level 3:* Unobservable inputs (including an entity's own data) using a market participant's perspective.

Valuation techniques frequently include inputs from several levels; the ranking of the conclusion is determined by the lowest level of significant inputs. As certain disclosures are required only for Level 3 inputs, it is important to carefully identify values obtained from them.

Practical Expedient

The framework offers a practical expedient for dealing with a large number of similar assets (e.g., debt securities) for which quoted prices in active markets are available but not readily accessible. It allows fair value to be measured by an alternative method provided that the entity demonstrates that it reasonably replicates actual prices.

Observable, Market-Based Inputs

Methods for measuring fair value should maximize observable, market-based inputs regardless of the approach adopted; inputs include reported prices, volatility measures, specific and broad credit data, liquidity statistics, and any other factors that have a significant effect on fair value. Determining what is observable market data requires considerable judgment; it includes prices or quotes from exchanges or traded markets that have sufficient liquidity and activity (e.g., Hong Kong, London, NASDAQ, New York, or Shanghai stock exchanges; Chicago, New York, or Tokyo commodities exchanges), as well as proxy market data that is proven to be highly correlated and has a logical, economic relationship with the asset involved. Judgment must be based on the strength of the evidence.

Observable data is:

- *Not proprietary.* Data from external sources is available to and regularly used by participants in the relevant market/product sector as a basis for transactions or verifying quotations.
- *Readily available.* Market participants are able to obtain access for a reasonable fee.
- *Regularly distributed.* Data is available in a timely enough manner to be used in pricing decisions; it is important to verify that changes between intervals have not occurred that would render the data less meaningful.
- *Available from multiple sources.* Data should be obtainable from more than one independent source, such as broker quotes and pricing services for financial instruments.
- *Transparent.* Sources providing or distributing the data and their role in a particular product/market are known to be reliable.
- *Verifiable.* Users can verify the data with the provider.

Market-based data is:

- *Reliable.* It reflects actual market parameters and is subject to periodic testing and controls. Entities should test and review the reliability of a source's data on an ongoing basis before actually using it for fair values.
- *Based on consensus.* Data from multiple sources should be comparable, with each verifying the others, within a reasonably narrow range.
- *From actively involved sources.* Data should originate from an active participant with respect to the relevant item in the applicable market.
- *Supported by actual trading.* Although the data need not be traced directly to a live transaction, there should be evidence that the information is drawn from real deals or used to price actual trades.

Even if inputs are based on observable data, the models that incorporate them must be reviewed and reassessed on an ongoing basis. Obviously available inputs may affect the choice of valuation technique. When Level 1 inputs are available, a market method normally provides better evidence of fair value than an income method.

Subsequent Events

Fair value reflects only facts and circumstances that existed on the specified date, as well as events occurring previously or which were reasonably foreseeable on that day. In some situations, significant events may occur after the close of a market but before the measurement date—for example, over a weekend. However, any aftermarket prices relating to this may not be representative due to lack of participants. Policies for identifying and incorporating such events affecting fair values need to be consistent. If an entity adjusts the quoted price, the measurement is Level 2.

 ## STAGE 6: ESTIMATE FAIR VALUE CONCLUSIONS

The result of the market determination process and the application of appropriate valuation methods will be fair value. When the conclusion applies to an asset group valued "in combination," the total is allocated to each item based on the specific facts and circumstances.

As the range of fair values by most valuation techniques can be relatively wide—normally around ± 5%, but in some circumstances ± 10%—fair value

TABLE 3.2 Ascendo, Inc. June 30, 2011 Fair Value Balance Sheets

	Approach	Low	High
Assets		($)	($)
Current			
Cash	Cost	20,614	20,614
Receivables	Income	1,364,000	1,391,000
Inventory	Cost	234,000	239,000
Prepaids	Cost	13,640	13,640
		1,632,254	1,664,254
Physical			
Land	Market	265,000	275,000
Building	Market	1,335,000	1,375,000
Plant	Cost	640,000	650,000
Equipment	Cost	135,000	140,000
Vehicles	Market	95,000	100,000
		2,470,000	2,540,000
Intangibles			
Technology	Income	170,000	190,000
Customer relationships	Income	375,000	415,000
Trade mark (name)	Income	210,000	235,000
Assembled workforce	Cost	155,000	170,000
		910,000	1,010,000
Goodwill	Residual	183,879	36,879
		5,196,133	5,251,133
Liabilities			
Bank overdraft		170,210	170,210
Payables & accruals		865,923	865,923
Mortgage	Income	635,000	665,000
		1,671,133	1,701,133
Fair Value		3,525,000	3,550,000

conclusions are conventionally rounded, always in thousands of dollars (unless nominal) and usually to the closet $5,000 or, for larger amounts, to roughly 1%. For example, an income approach fair value of $3,231,000 for a cash-generating unit would be rounded to $3,225,000 or $3,250,000 as applicable.

In purchase price allocations where the totals have to be reconciled to the actual consideration, it is often helpful for the valuator to establish ranges for each asset class and work with management to select the most appropriate amounts within them for each item. Table 3.2 provides an example. The assembled workforce is treated as part of goodwill for reporting purposes.

CHAPTER FOUR

Taming the Future

There is nothing wrong with change, if it is in the right direction.

—*Winston Spencer Churchill (1874–1965), British statesman*

C HAPTER 3 DEALT WITH THE FRAMEWORK for establishing fair values. Those, like all forms of value, are based on what is expected to happen. This chapter covers what management can do to tame the future. It makes its best guesses in budgets, forecasts, and business plans for presentations to staff, directors, analysts, and investors. But none of those give fair values, which are based not on what management anticipates, but on what market participants expect. Although many practitioners use budget figures for the current year as a base, reference should be made to analysts' reports on comparables whenever possible. This practice tends to limit expected growth to that of the industry as a whole and probably will reflect a reversion to the mean, rather than a continuation of past favorable trends.

When a turnaround is involved, market participants tend to be pessimistic, expecting more time, greater investment, and lower returns than management does. Alternatively, they can be overly enthusiastic, willing to pay what may appear to be excessive premiums for growth.

One measure used by analysts is the price/earnings to growth (PEG) ratio. If an entity has a price to earnings ratio (PER) of 12.5 times based on reported profit of the latest 12 months (LTM) and excellent projected earnings growth of 7.5% a year, the PEG ratio is 1.67 times (12.5/7.5); anything under 2.0 times is usually considered reasonable. If the growth were to accelerate to 12.0%, the PER could rise to 20 times (capitalization rate of 5.0%) with the PEG still remaining at 1.67 times. If growth were to fall to 4.5% and the PER stayed unchanged, the PEG would become 2.77 times. In eras of high investor enthusiasm, market participants have paid PEGs of up to 5.5 times, occasionally even more. At that level, with only 4.5% annual growth, the PER would be about 25 times (a capitalization rate of only 4.0%).

 DEFINITIONS

Most readers know of budgets and business plans, and some are familiar with forecasts and projections, but it may help to define them. They all involve prospective financial information, the name used by accountants and valuators for material referring to future rather than past periods.

Budgets

A budget is a financial document distinguished by its time frame (by months typically, normally not more than a year) and level of detail (usually from the bottom up by activities, branches, and departments). It is normally integrated with general ledger accounts so as to allow easy comparisons with actual amounts.

Business Plans

A business plan is a formal statement of operating and financial goals, setting out the reason they are considered attainable, the additional resources (financial, human, and physical) necessary to achieve them, and the detailed means of realizing them. The planning process looks further into the future than a budget does, commonly three to five years, allowing management to consider alternative strategies. In many cases, the process of reviewing the outlook for the three facets of a business (existing operations, emerging activities, and future opportunities) is as important as the resulting document.

From the point of its fair value, it is essential that a business separate the three facets and remove from existing operations all costs and revenues, if any, relating to the other two. Emerging activities cover internal start-ups, new product launches, entries into additional markets, or any other situation that has commenced but has not yet reached stability. Future opportunities are represented by items in R&D until completion of the test market phase.

Forecasts

A financial forecast is a set of prospective financial statements that present, to the best of the preparer's knowledge and belief, an entity's expected financial position, results of operations, and cash flows for a number of future periods; frequently this is by quarters for the first two years and then annually for the next three or more. Financial forecasts build on the latest available historical data and adopt the preparer's view (usually management's) of the most likely assumptions relating to the conditions anticipated to occur and the course of action expected to be taken. They are normally single-point estimates but may also be expressed as ranges.

Projections

Financial projections are sets of prospective financial statements that present an entity's financial position, results of operations, and cash flows using not the assumptions that management deems most likely but hypothetical ones that are reasonably possible.

When using scenarios, discussed later in this chapter, most of the prospective financial information is in the form of projections. As fair value involves the use of market participants' assumptions rather than those of management, the figures underlying them are always projections rather than forecasts, although for the early periods they may be the same as the budget or business plans adopted by management. A frequent use of projections is considering what-if situations.

 ## EFFECT OF MARKET PARTICIPANTS' ASSUMPTIONS

Choosing market participants' rather than management's basic assumptions about growth in sales and margin improvements of a business will have a significant effect on value. To demonstrate this we compare the two sets of outlooks for Panther Inc. Table 4.1 sets out a simplified financial forecast based on management's expected conditions and anticipated courses of action, together with other related assumptions given to the board of directors in early 2011.

TABLE 4.1   Panther Inc. Financial Forecast—Management's Expectations
($ millions)

		2010 (Actual)	2011 (Forecast)	2012 (Forecast)	2013 (Forecast)	2014 (Forecast)	2015 (Forecast)
Sales		522.4	556.4	592.5	631.0	672.1	715.7
Growth		5.8%	6.5%	6.5%	6.5%	6.5%	6.5%
Pretax profit		37.613	42.839	48.587	54.900	61.829	65.847
Margin		7.2%	7.7%	8.2%	8.7%	9.2%	9.2%
Income tax	33%	(12.412)	(14.137)	(16.034)	(18.117)	(20.403)	(21.730)
Net income		25.201	28.702	32.553	36.783	41.425	44.118
Growth			13.9%	13.4%	13.0%	12.6%	6.5%
Net income		25.201	28.702	32.553	36.783	41.425	44.118
Depreciation	3.4%	17.762	18.916	20.146	21.455	22.850	24.335
Capital expenditures		(26.000)	(10.000)	(24.000)	(18.000)	(22.000)	(25.000)
Working capital	12.6%	(3.604)	(4.278)	(4.557)	(4.853)	(5.168)	(5.504)
Cash flow		13.359	33.340	24.142	35.385	37.107	37.949
Growth			149.6%	−27.6%	46.6%	4.9%	2.3%

However, market participants do not totally agree. A major investment study of the industry shows growth at only 5.3% annually for the next five years, made up of 3% volume increases and 2.3% inflation. While acknowledging that major improvements in margins are likely, it places them at 30 basis points (bp) annually for three years, rather than management's 50 bp for four years. Using such market participants' assumptions leads to a good but less stellar performance, as shown in Table 4.2.

After five years, there is a 5.5% shortfall in sales, a 13.7% decrease in net income, and a 8.4% drop in cash flow under the market participants' views. With respect to the value of the firm, the hit is even greater. If the industry sells at a PER of 13.2 times (equivalent to a capitalization rate of 7.6%) with 5.3% anticipated future long-term growth in net income (no further margin improvement), the implied industry discount rate is 12.9% (7.6% + 5.3%). Both management and market participants assume that over the six years (one actual, five future), capital expenditures will equal depreciation, which is planned to continue to run at the same 3.4% of revenues as in 2010. Working

TABLE 4.2 Panther Inc. Financial Projections—Market Participants' Assumptions ($ millions)

		2010 (Actual)	2011 (Projection)	2012 (Projection)	2013 (Projection)	2014 (Projection)	2015 (Projection)
Sales		522.4	550.1	579.2	609.9	642.3	676.3
Growth			5.3%	5.3%	5.3%	5.3%	5.3%
Pretax profit		37.613	41.257	45.181	49.405	53.951	56.810
Margin		7.2%	7.5%	7.8%	8.1%	8.4%	8.4%
Income tax	33%	(12.412)	(13.615)	(14.910)	(16.304)	(17.804)	(18.747)
Net income		25.201	27.642	30.271	33.102	36.147	38.063
Growth			9.7%	9.5%	9.3%	9.2%	5.3%
Net income		25.201	27.642	30.271	33.102	36.147	38.063
Depreciation	3.4%	17.762	18.703	19.694	20.738	21.837	22.994
Capital expenditures		(26.000)	(10.000)	(24.000)	(18.000)	(22.000)	(22.000)
Working capital	12.6%	(3.604)	(3.489)	(3.673)	(3.868)	(4.073)	(4.289)
Cash flow		13.359	32.856	22.292	31.971	31.911	34.768
			146.0%	−32.2%	43.4%	−0.2%	9.0%

capital requirements in each year are 12.6% of the projected sales increase (see Tables 4.3 and 4.4).

Thus the investment value under management's assumptions is $522 million, compared with a fair value of $403 million using those of market participants. This is a decrease of 23%, as shown in Table 4.5.

SCENARIO ANALYSIS

Another process that market participants consider is scenario analysis. Today, past trends are not likely to be as good a predictor of the future as they were previously thought to be. The world is no longer a series of loosely connected, reasonably predictable economic relationships; it is now an interconnected web through which the global impact of local events may be felt almost instantaneously. In response to uncertainty, scenario analysis is being widely used by many organizations, large and small, concerned with volatile situations. It is a way of taming the future by incorporating into financial projections

TABLE 4.3 Panther Inc. Discounted Cash Flow (DCF) Values—Management's Assumptions ($ millions)

		2010	2011	2012	2013	2014	2015
Cash flow		13.359	33.340	24.142	35.385	37.107	37.949
Compounding factor	12.9%		1.0645	1.2018	1.3569	1.5319	1.7295
Present values			31.320	20.088	26.079	24.223	21.942
Net income							44.118
Discount rate	12.9%						
Growth rate	−6.5%						
Capitalization rate	6.4%						
Capitalized net income							689.341
Compounding factor							1.7295
Total present values		123.652	Terminal amount		398.577	Intrinsic value	522.229

TABLE 4.4 Panther Inc. DCF Value—Market Participants' Assumptions ($ millions)

		2010	2011	2012	2013	2014	2015
Cash flow		13.359	32.856	22.292	31.971	31.911	34.768
Compounding factor	12.9%		1.0645	1.2018	1.3569	1.5319	1.7295
Present values			30.865	18.548	23.563	20.831	20.103
Net income							38.063
Discount rate	12.9%						
Growth rate	−5.3%						
Capitalization rate	7.6%						
Capitalized net income							500.824
Compounding factor							1.7295
Total present values		113.911	Terminal amount		289.577	Fair value	403.488

TABLE 4.5 Panther Inc.—Comparison DCF Values ($ millions)

Assumptions	Total Present Values	Terminal Amount	Intrinsic/Fair Value
Management's	123.652	398.577	522.229
Market participants'	113.911	289.577	403.488
Reduction	–7.9%	–27.3%	–22.7%

management's or market participants' understanding of forces such as demographics, globalization, technological change, and environmental sustainability that are shaping the future. While scenario analysis originated with strategic decisions, many entities apply the techniques to operations as a means of assessing their outcomes under alternative views of the future.

All scenarios follow the same basic methodology focusing largely on answering four questions: What could happen? What would be the impact on the business? How should we respond? How probable are the events? Figure 4.1 sets out the six stages of the process.

Before embarking on a scenario analysis, it is essential to be clear about what market participants want addressed, their (not just management's) anticipated uncertainties about the future, and the scope and time frames for the scenarios. Four broad types of issues are frequently considered:

1. *Social:* For example, high unemployment
2. *Economic:* The impact of $150-per-barrel oil
3. *Political:* Middle East uprisings
4. *Technological:* Changing use of smart phones and social media

When management has agreed on all issues to be covered and the scope and time frames are defined, they should be documented and compared with what can be ascertained as to the views of market participants. This often involves a strengths, weaknesses, opportunities, and threats (SWOT) review of the firm. Applied judiciously, scenario analysis can provide valuable insights to how the future might unfold, thereby enabling organizations to react with greater speed, agility, and confidence.

The main objective of preparing a set of financial projection scenarios is to identify a broader range of possible future outcomes for the business, not just a single set showing illusory certainty. For valuation purposes, the three scenarios developed for the First Chicago method are recommended: success

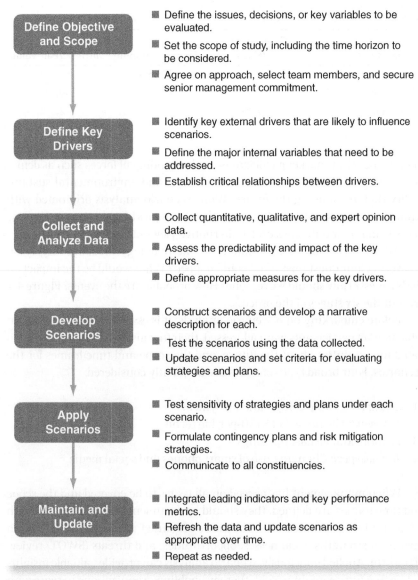

Define Objective and Scope
- Define the issues, decisions, or key variables to be evaluated.
- Set the scope of study, including the time horizon to be considered.
- Agree on approach, select team members, and secure senior management commitment.

Define Key Drivers
- Identify key external drivers that are likely to influence scenarios.
- Define the major internal variables that need to be addressed.
- Establish critical relationships between drivers.

Collect and Analyze Data
- Collect quantitative, qualitative, and expert opinion data.
- Assess the predictability and impact of the key drivers.
- Define appropriate measures for the key drivers.

Develop Scenarios
- Construct scenarios and develop a narrative description for each.
- Test the scenarios using the data collected.
- Update scenarios and set criteria for evaluating strategies and plans.

Apply Scenarios
- Test sensitivity of strategies and plans under each scenario.
- Formulate contingency plans and risk mitigation strategies.
- Communicate to all constituencies.

Maintain and Update
- Integrate leading indicators and key performance metrics.
- Refresh the data and update scenarios as appropriate over time.
- Repeat as needed.

FIGURE 4.1 Scenario Planning Process

Source: Management Accounting Guideline, *Scenario Planning: Plotting a Course through an Uncertain World* (AICPA, CMA Canada, and CIMA, 2010).

(management's most likely view), survival (poorer performance, considering the probable views of market participants), and status quo (continuing the current situation, possibly borderline failure).

Preparing the scenarios' financial projections requires:

- Analyzing the financial implications of alternative strategies
- Testing the sensitivity of key assumptions, financial measures, and variables
- Developing alternative financial plans and forecasts
- Defining performance measures and leading indicators to track potential triggers and key drivers
- Monitoring and reporting internal and external performance indicators likely to impact current and planned strategies

Whether any specific projection actually turns out to be accurate is only part of the picture—as the saying goes, even a broken clock is right twice a day. The task is to map probable outcomes and their related uncertainties. In a world where actions taken now have a significant influence on the future, uncertainties often give rise to opportunities. All scenario financial projections should be supported by articulated and defensible logic. The user must understand enough of the process involved to make an independent assessment of their quality and to properly understand the individual opportunities and risks. The wise consumer is not a trusting bystander, but a participant and a critic. Every decision maker ultimately has to rely on his or her own intuition and judgment.

Effective, well-prepared scenarios can help narrow the areas where action is required and should:

- Provide an essential context
- Reveal overlooked possibilities
- Expose unexamined implicit assumptions

 ## SCENARIO IMPLICATIONS

Scenario planning is not just a one-off exercise. Assume that six months after the scenarios were completed, oil reached $200 a barrel and the G-20 countries imposed strict mandates on CO_2 emissions within five years? The entity in Table 4.6 would have had to revisit its plans and might focus on only two scenarios: "Do It or Die" and "Cost of Doing Business." After more detailed modeling, it

TABLE 4.6 Comparison of Four Scenarios

	Do It or Die	Competitive Advantage	Cost of Doing Business	Steady as She Goes
Approach to Innovation	The minimum is not enough; must be the best to win.	Innovative leadership has real value.	Must meet the standards; little advantage in being a leader.	Focus on select areas where there is strong demand.
Marketing Strategies	Either be the safe option (compliant) or be the best.	Must be a leader.	Partner with builders to secure share.	Be No. 1 in select niches.
Market Goals	Own the high end.	Acquire share.	Be the preferred supplier.	Build share in niches.
Financial Goals	Achieve high margins.	Focus on size and scale.	Be a low-cost producer.	Achieve modest growth over time.

could decide to concentrate on delivering solutions that exceed the mandated minimums while keeping prices reasonable. Well-articulated scenarios allow for fast, confident decisions by providing a sound basis for evaluating the impact of changing market conditions.

It is essential to constantly review actual and projected results against the scenarios so management can act quickly when it sees any changes in the market that may impact performance. As organizations struggle to deal with an increasingly uncertain world, scenarios can help in understanding the choices, opportunities, and implications that uncertainty presents.

The Future

More and more businesses either have scrapped formal budgets or, while continuing to develop them, manage the businesses using rolling forecasts, flexible budgets, and event-driven planning. Using nineteenth-century tools to manage a twenty-first-century entity in a volatile global economy often does not make sense.

In 2010 Accenture surveyed 273 companies with respect to their planning capabilities; only 11% were fully satisfied, compared with 17% in 2008 and 20% in 2000. This reality was underscored by the recession, which saw many budgets fail due to economic volatility, rising commodity prices, and fluctuating exchanges rates. More than two-thirds of respondents said their planning accuracy had diminished because of economic volatility, while 81% intended to try to improve forecasting performance.

Key Performance Indicators

Most businesses have a few key performance indicators (KPIs). These may be simple, such as a percentage of on-time deliveries, or as complex as Six Sigma values. However, definitions vary from industry to industry, even firm to firm. Benchmarking, a significant part of performance input, is difficult without standard definitions.

In 2011, the Gartner Group Inc. and the Enhanced Business Reporting Consortium (EBRC) joined the World Intellectual Capital Initiative (WICI), XBRL International, and a number of companies and financial institutions to develop "voluntary industry standard measures that are predictive of corporate performance." The concept is to develop competencies and capabilities in the areas being measured and harvest the benefits.

The proposed metrics for all industries are set out in Table 4.7. The AICPA website has links that allow visitors to view the makeup of each metric.

TABLE 4.7   Proposed KPIs

Business Domain	Aggregates		Prime Metrics		
Demand Management	Market Responsive-ness	Target Market Index	Market Coverage Index	Market Share Index	Opportunity/ Threat Index
		Product Portfolio Index	Channel Profitability Index	Con-figurability Index	
	Sales Effectiveness	Sales Opportunity Index	Sales Cycle Index	Sales Close Index	Sales Price Index
		Cost of Sales Index	Forecast Accuracy	Customer Retention Index	
	Product Development Effectiveness	New Products Index	Feature Function Index	Time to Market Index	R&D Success Index
Supply Management	Customer Responsive-ness	On-Time Delivery	Order Fill Rate	Material Quality	Service Accuracy
		Service Performance	Customer Care Per-formance	Agreement Effective-ness	Transformation Ratio

(continued)

TABLE 4.7 *(Continued)*

Business Domain	Aggregates	Prime Metrics			
	Supplier Effectiveness	Supplier On-Time Delivery	Supplier Order Fill Rate	Supplier Material Quality	Supplier Service Accuracy
		Supplier Service Performance	Supplier Care Performance	Supplier Agreement Effectiveness	Supplier Transformation Ratio
	Operational Efficiency	Cash to Cash Cycle Time	Conversion Cost	Asset Utilization	Sigma Value
Support Services	Human Resources Responsiveness	Recruitment Effectiveness Index	Benefits Administration Index	Skills Inventory Index	Employee Training Index
		HR Advisory Index	HR Total Cost Index		
	Information Technology Responsiveness	Systems Performance	IT Support Performance	Partnership Ratio	Service Level Effectiveness
		New Projects Index	IT Total Cost Index		
	Finance & Regulatory Responsiveness	Compliance Index	Accuracy Index	Advisory Index	Cost of Service Index

Source: American Institute of CPAs, "Gartner/EBRC KPI Initiative." www.aicpa.org/interestareas/frc/accountingfinancialreporting/enhancedbusinessreporting/pages/gartnerebrckpiinitiative.aspx.

CHAPTER FIVE

Projecting What Is to Come

> It's tough to make predictions, especially about the future.
>
> —*Lawrence Peter "Yogi" Berra (1925–), American athlete*

N OW WE COME TO THE REALLY INTERESTING PART: preparing effective supportable financial projections for fair values. This is always an iterative process, as the projections must reflect the assumptions of market participants, which are not directly known, rather than the anticipations of management. It involves generating hypotheses about outcomes and eventual responses, discovering avoidable unpleasant surprises, and identifying otherwise missed opportunities. As the projections will be audited, it is essential that management assumes responsibility for the reasonableness of:

- The underlying assumptions
- Their context and structure
- The logic and integrity of the model used
- The resulting amounts

This chapter covers the major problems of financial property concerning:

- *Context:* Base the future on the past.
- *Structure:* The truth is in the parts.
- *Models:* Avoid unnecessary risks.
- *Assumptions:* Garbage in, garbage out.
- *Results:* Achieve believable and supportable conclusions.

 ## BASE THE FUTURE ON THE PAST

An understanding of the context, especially the economic outlook, is essential in preparing a financial projection. According to Marshall McLuhan (1911–1980), a Canadian philosopher, "Too often people steer their way into the future while staring into the rearview mirror because the past is so much more comforting than the present."

Used properly, such a rear view is an extraordinarily powerful forecasting tool. Past events can help connect the dots of present indicators. Consider the uncertainty after the 2000 tech crash. A few newcomers, such as Google, Yahoo, Vodafone, and Facebook, emerged triumphant; most traditional telecommunications companies, TV networks, and print media suffered. The changes were hard to categorize, much less predict. If, however, one looked back as far as the early 1950s when TV took off, catalyzing a new mass-media structure, the late 1990s showed eerie parallels to that era. The world is now at a moment when an old mass-media order is being replaced by a new personal-media one, with everyone struggling to understand and adjust. History can be a guide, provided that one avoids the common predilection for assuming certainty and continuity that leads to wrong conclusions.

The most recent past is rarely a reliable indicator of the future; if it were, any of us could successfully predict share prices. Markets do not behave that way, nor do any other trends. Do not ignore turns when looking at the straight. A valuator looks back to identify patterns; for parallels it is desirable to go back at least twice as far as you plan to project. Ten years of the past to five of the future is a reasonable mix. As Mark Twain (1836–1910), the American humorist, is said to have commented: "History doesn't repeat itself, at best it sometimes rhymes."

It is essential to avoid the temptation to use the past the way a drunk uses a lamppost—for support, rather than for illumination.

Continuity

Another part of the context of a financial projection is continuity. To be meaningful, it must be firmly based on actual historical results. This is usually done by analyzing in detail past financial statements after necessary adjustments, looking at trends over time in major factors, such as revenues, costs, assets, and liabilities, as well as in standard ratios such as profit margins and various liquidity indicators. The latter sets present a useful picture of management's reactions to external developments and events. The analytical procedures chosen should be designed to identify relationships and to pinpoint unusual items that may be indications of possible changes in the business. The most common consist of comparing:

- Current financial information with that of previous periods
- Actual past results with comparable budgets or forecasts
- Amounts or ratios with expectations developed by management
- Projected ratios with industry averages or those of similar publicly traded companies

S-Curves

Change is not linear. Part of a projection's context is variations in the rate of change, as very little unfolds in a straight line. Important developments typically follow an S-curve, starting slowly and incrementally, puttering along quietly, then suddenly exploding, before eventually tapering off. One famous S-curve is Moore's law, which states that the density of circuits on a silicon wafer doubles every 18 months.

Every computer user continues to benefit from this 1965 insight; the top of the S is nowhere in sight. Eventually it will flatten, certainly with regard to silicon chips; in a broader form (density regardless of the material), this law is likely to remain in effect.

S-curves are fractal in nature—a large, broadly defined trench, usually composed of several smaller, more precisely defined ones. Discovering an emerging S-curve may indicate that a larger, more important one is lurking in the background. Miss that, and the firm's strategy might amount to standing on a whale, fishing for tadpoles. A significant part of forecasting is to identify emerging S-curves well ahead of the inflection points. These are dramatic moments of change. When anticipating them, professionals may do worse than the public.

Observers glimpsing the beginnings of an S-curve frequently miscalculate its time frame; there is a common tendency to overestimate the short-term effects (which are often immediately apparent) and underestimate the long-term implications. Visionaries may conclude that the revolution will arrive next year; when reality fails to conform, disappointment leads to the conclusion that it will never occur (right before it arrives).

We are all by nature linear thinkers; beware of underestimating the speed of changes. Phenomena governed by exponential growth catch us by surprise. Some instinctively draw a straight line through the S-curve, forgetting the lag at the start and missing the period of explosive growth, even though we may arrive at the same end. According to William Gibson (1948–), a British author, "The future's already arrived. It's just not evenly distributed yet."

Opportunities are frequently different from those predicted by the majority; even the most anticipated futures tend to arrive in unexpected ways. In the early 1980s, personal computer makers expected that every home would soon have one for word processing and spreadsheets. When that event finally came about, though, it was actually driven by entertainment, not work. One of the best ways to spot an emerging S-curve is to become attuned to things that don't fit. Find something that may come whistling in out of the blue in the near future; look for smart ideas that seem to have gone nowhere.

 ## THE TRUTH IS IN THE PARTS

Normally, the whole of a business is valued; however, in making financial projections, it is better to look at each part rather than just the whole. Virtually all entities have more than one function; they behave in different ways. Most successful businesses have at least two, and preferably all, of the following facets, which were mentioned in Chapter 4: several existing operations, emerging activities, and future opportunities (the last being the future of the entity). Emerging activities are businesses that either are or are about to be generating revenues. Future opportunities are research and development (R&D) or marketing projects. According to Alfred Pritchard Sloan (1875–1966), the first CEO of General Motors, who made the company number one in the industry, "It is better to cannibalize yourself than have others do it."

In many cases, existing operations cover more than one activity with different sales cycles and profitability. Often losses are locked away beyond the outsider's gaze and found only by disaggregation. The importance of this process is

TABLE 5.1 Anaconda Electronics Inc. Comparative Income Statements ($ thousands)

Income Statement	2003	2004	2005	2006	2007	2008
Revenue						
Services	127,824	130,378	127,581	127,198	133,826	142,341
Equipment	81,262	72,868	77,473	52,198	0	0
	209,086	203,246	205,054	179,396	133,826	142,341
Services growth	1.5%	2.0%	−2.1%	−0.3%	5.2%	6.4%
Gross Profit						
Services	30,544	31,152	32,439	32,273	29,220	32,039
Equipment	18,995	16,087	16,812	11,536	0	0
	49,539	47,239	49,251	43,809	29,220	32,039
Services gross margin	23.9%	23.9%	25.4%	25.4%	21.8%	22.5%
Expenses						
Administration	23,975	22,339	24,756	24,321	15,125	15,777
Selling and engineering	18,258	19,089	17,317	15,496	5,257	6,190
Corporate charges	2,539	3,588	3,917	3,903	2,841	2,160
	44,772	45,016	45,990	43,720	23,223	24,127
Pretax Profit	4,767	2,223	3,261	89	5,997	7,912
Income Tax	(1,311)	(714)	(1,023)	(24)	(1,792)	(2,650)
Reported Net Income	3,456	1,509	2,238	65	4,205	5,262
Tax rate	27.5%	32.1%	31.4%	27.0%	29.9%	33.5%
Continuing Business	4,302	4,648	5,096	4,319	4,141	5,262
Discontinued Functions	(846)	(3,139)	(2,858)	(4,254)	64	0
	3,456	1,509	2,238	65	4,205	5,262

demonstrated by an analysis of Anaconda Electronics Inc., supplying the telephone industry, as shown in Tables 5.1 and 5.2.

From 2003 to its sale in 2006, Anaconda's equipment supply activities, shown as Discontinued Functions, lost $11,097,000; thereafter, the firm relied wholly on services. Disaggregation of the continuing businesses shows that their defense contract was overzealously bid in 2005, resulting in continuing losses until it expired in mid-2010, when the firm was granted a two-year extension with a 20% price increase. For financial projections to be meaningful, each activity (segment) should be projected independently, as well as valued separately.

TABLE 5.2   Anaconda Electronics Inc. 2006 Activity Income Statements ($ thousands)

	Total	Defense	Commercial	Services	Instruments
Continuing Business Revenue	127,198	36,832	76,989	113,821	13,377
Gross Profit	32,273	97	25,515	25,612	6,661
Gross margin	25.4%	0.3%	33.1%	22.5%	49.8%
Expenses					
Administration	17,624	5,633	10,689	16,322	1,302
Selling and engineering	5,926	291	4,428	4,719	1,207
Corporate charges	2,803	626	1,336	1,962	841
	26,353	6,550	16,453	23,003	3,350
Pretax Profit	5,920	(6,453)	9,062	2,609	3,311
Income Tax	(1,601)	1,742	(2,447)	(705)	(896)
Net Income	4,319	(4,711)	6,615	1,904	2,415
Tax rate	27.0%	27.0%	27.0%	27.0%	27.1%
Net Margin	3.4%	–12.8%	8.6%	1.7%	18.1%

Sources of Profits Are Important

Ask anyone who is not an accountant, and even some who are, about cost accounting. Their eyes glaze over and they wonder what that boring activity has to do with value. An analysis of where a business earns its profits and which products or customers are reducing the bottom line is important. For example, a small manufacturing company once discovered that its best-selling product line was eating away at profits that otherwise could fund the firm's future, even though the financial statements showed the business overall was a nice moneymaker. This was determined when, as part of preparing the firm for sale, management introduced activity-based costing (ABC). Until then, they had no idea that a substantial portion of administrative expenses was attributable solely to supporting that particular line.

Any entity being valued that sells more than a dozen or so products, achieves annual sales growth of more than 10% and has customers with widely divergent buying patterns is likely to have some products or customers that are sapping its strength and reducing its value. It is essential to find and fix them.

Economic Value Generated

Many managers use some form of economic value generated (EVG), such as Economic Value Added (EVA®), a proprietary tool owned by Stern Stewart & Company of New York, to establish bonuses and assess capital projects. In simple terms, EVG is the difference between earnings before interest after notional tax (EBIAT) and a capital charge; this is usually total invested capital (both debt and equity) multiplied by weighted average cost of capital (WACC). Various studies have shown that a number of public companies have a negative EVG—one reason that their business activities do not create additional value for shareholders.

During 1999, a major European engineering organization announced at a shareholders' meeting that it expected to have a positive EVG by 2001. It actually took until 2005, well after the end of the post-Internet bubble, to be achieved. During the turnaround, its shares outperformed the general stock market. Studies have shown the same effect for U.S. firms using EVG as a management tool. One useful function of a valuator is to help a firm's management enhance the position of its owners.

Whether a company is a software developer or a cheese manufacturer, an early projection step is to use a simplified form of ABC to determine the profitability of product and customer groups. Once management has determined how to deal with loss-making areas, it should establish the EVG of the profitable segments. This requires determining the capital involved in those products and customers, as well as the proportions funded by debt and equity. From those figures, an appropriate capital charge is calculated and the EVG is determined for each activity.

AVOID UNNECESSARY RISKS

Spreadsheets are cheap, versatile, and used by millions of people every day. They are, however, difficult to audit and clumsy to work with in collaborative, repetitive processes such as budgeting or preparing financial projections—we "can't live with them, but can't live without them." Good spreadsheet management involves specialized software to be effective and complete. Excel has tools for auditing, tracking, and controlling changes, but they must not be relied on completely; simple add-ons make it easier to track and spot changes, detect unauthorized or inaccurate modifications, or determine which cells need checking. It doesn't matter which one you use. "Don't leave home without it."

Criticality, the likely impact of an error occurring in a spreadsheet, has three levels:

Low: No key business decisions are made based on the information, data, or conclusions.

Middling: An error or a delay in preparation may result in significant loss, or information in it may be sensitive.

High: An error or a delay in preparation may result in a material loss, or information in it is highly sensitive.

Inherent risk is defined by the Institute of Internal Auditors as "the risk to an organization in the absence of any actions management might take to alter either the risk's probability or impact."

A spreadsheet's inherent risk is a combination of its criticality and the likelihood of error. The latter is derived from a combination of its complexity and its design. The complexity depends on size; difficulty of formulas; volume of linkages to other cells, tabs, and spreadsheets; amount of data; and existence of macros or other code. I recommend using software that automatically scans spreadsheets and scores them for complexity.

Projecting Revenues

Many cost figures are established as percentages of revenues; therefore, projecting those amounts is one of the most important functions in preparing prospective financial information. There are two basic methods: bottom up or top down. The former starts with customers, volumes, and prices through the various sales channels; the latter fits trends to historical data, normally by business unit.

Bottom Up

Product and service organizations are structured and managed differently. For best results, make separate projections for volumes and prices. In some industries (for example, computers), effective prices go down all the time. All services, products, and customers have life cycles with a beginning (birth) and end (death), which must be taken into account when projecting the effects of strategies that include various stages of maturity, all of which have an impact on future revenues. To effectively plan for growth, a business must analyze those by markets, units, and products.

Top Down

Sales are developed using statistical tools to project trends in historical data. Excel can calculate six types of trend lines: linear, logarithmic, polynomial, geometric, exponential, and moving average. For the first five, it will project the results out into the future and display the relevant mathematical formulas. At least five years of historical data are needed for trend line analyses, but adding more will provide increasingly better results. The quality of the fit (high R^2) between the data plotted against time and the trend line drawn through it is important.

The most common trend, a linear one, is simply a straight line, calculated so that the sum of the squares of the differences between the trend and the data is as small as possible (known as a "least squares fit"). It is represented by the equation $y = mx + b$, with m being the slope and b being the intercept on the x-axis. Such trends, which can be up, down, or level, are most useful when an entity's past results have been relatively consistent and are expected to continue in a similar fashion.

Even if the regression line has an excellent statistical fit, the resulting projections may not be reasonable. In many cases, a second-order polynomial regression can have a near perfect fit with the past 10 years' sales but may result in implausible projections showing revenues rising or falling rapidly. Therefore, caution is recommended in relying only on trends.

Historical Income Statements

An analysis of historical income statements will give a range of percentages of sales for every category of expenses, such as labor, material, and overhead, which form cost of sales. In general, the most plausible methods are to use the last three-year averages of such percentages or to apply a Monte Carlo simulation using random amounts in the established ranges.

Assumptions

Assumptions materially affect all financial projections. With any model, the quality of the conclusions completely depends on the quality of the assumptions. Everyone involved must ensure that they are reasonable, reliable, and consistent with existing market information, the current economic climate, and past experience. Key external and internal nonfinancial performance indicators, such as market share and customer satisfaction, must be taken into account.

Caution

Management spends a great deal of time in developing (the most likely) financial forecasts. In some cases they resemble a hockey stick, with revenues, margins, and net incomes all increasing rapidly. In that case, look out; everything will not go as management expects. The user, as critic, must distinguish between the possible and various degrees of probable. In such an event, applying various scenarios is essential (see Chapter 4).

Monte Carlo Simulations

In most financial projections, the outcome depends, to varying degrees, on different inputs. Minor changes in one of these, say gross margins, may have a significant effect at the net income level. One well-established way of dealing with this is a Monte Carlo simulation. The traditional discounted cash flows (DCF) method has limitations associated with imprecise treatment of risk and lack of information, due to being based on single-point estimates of the variables that drive projected revenues and costs. Monte Carlo simulations, by contrast, work well with numerous what-if situations and unknowns related to the future of a business or technology. They are particularly useful for valuing intangible assets or when the impact of multiple scenarios and unknowns would not be properly reflected in a standard spreadsheet or even a decision tree analysis.

Those simulations work best with inputs that have a reasonably narrow range of possible values. The starting point is to specify a probability band for each input (e.g., selling price, units sold, market share, etc.). Then establish their likely behavior (e.g., selling prices are equally likely within the band; units sold are more likely to be clustered in the lower end). Combined, they define the outputs from each of the thousands of iterations performed. The model randomly selects a value for each input using the band and likely distributions; it then calculates thousands of scenarios with different combinations of inputs. The results are a distribution of individual calculated outputs; their mean represents the most likely outcome.

Example: Monte Carlo Simulation

Consider a revenue forecast with the following assumptions:

Selling price: most likely $5.00 per unit, but could vary from $4.00 to $5.50
Units sold: most likely 1,000,000 plus or minus 10%, but could be as low as zero.

The spreadsheet answer would be: sales = unit price × unit sales = $5.00 × 1,000,000 = $5,000,000. However, there is a wide range of possibilities:

Best case: $5.50 × 1,100,000 = $6,050,000
Minimum likely case: $4.00 × 900,000 = $3,600,000
Worst case: $5.00 × 0 = $0

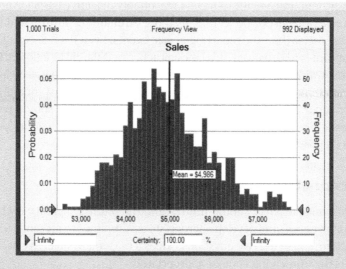

FIGURE 5.1 Monte Carlo Sales Histogram

Source: NACVA presentation Kennedy (2008).

The simulation recalculates the spreadsheet about 1,000 times, changing at random the selling price and units sold within their estimated bands. It then accumulates all the projections shown in Figure 5.1, calculating the mean ($4,986,000) as the most likely answer. This is only 0.3% below the spreadsheet result but is much more supportable, as the spreadsheet ignores the embedded risk that actual sales might be zero.

The statistics for this histogram are:

Trials: 1,000
Mean: $4,986,000
Median: $4,875,000
Standard deviation: $988,000

The power of Monte Carlo simulations to consider and account for potential variability of the inputs in a financial projection makes it a very useful tool. ▓

 ## GARBAGE IN, GARBAGE OUT

The quality of any financial projection depends on both the data available to support the assumptions adopted and the process involved. The AICPA *Guide for Prospective Financial Statements* requires a responsible party, normally a member of management, to have a reasonably objective basis for presenting a financial forecast or projection, as those estimate the future, and therefore are less precise than the reporting of past events. Even if a U.S. certified public accountant is not involved, this is best practice and should be followed by everyone. The *Guide* states that there will usually be differences between forecasted (projected) and actual results, because events and circumstances frequently do not occur as expected. Both forecasts and projections should present, to the best of the responsible party's knowledge and belief, the entity's expected financial positions, results of operation and cash flows.

Appropriate Assumptions

The responsible party should understand the required quality of the necessary information and develop appropriate assumptions to present a forecast or projection, satisfying two questions: "Does a reasonably objective basis exist?" and "Is the underlying context appropriate?"

In selecting assumptions, considerable judgment is required as well as knowledge of the business and an understanding of the industry in which it operates. Consider in particular:

- Can sufficient facts be obtained and informed judgments be made about past and future events or circumstances to support the underlying assumptions?
- Are any of the significant assumptions so subjective that no reasonably objective basis exists to present a forecast or projection?
- Would people knowledgeable in the entity's business and industry select any materially different assumptions?
- Is the length of the forecast or projection period appropriate?
- Which key factors have the greatest potential impact on the forecast or projection results?
- Which factors are significant matters of judgment?
- What are the responsible party's perceptions of the needs of a user?
- Could omission or misstatement of any assumptions change or influence the judgment of a user?

Seek out the best information that is reasonably available to develop the assumptions; spending on incremental information should be commensurate with the anticipated benefit. A projection may be easier to support if some of the assumptions and the conclusions are presented as ranges.

Deciding if suitable assumptions can be developed for each key factor is based on:

- Significance to the entity's business plans
- The financial importance and pervasiveness of the potential effect
- The impact on the conclusion or presentation of the forecast or projection

A rational relationship between the assumptions and the underlying facts and circumstances is essential; in particular they must be:

- Conformed to past, current, and expected conditions
- Complete
- Developed for each key factor
- Free of undue optimism or pessimism
- Consistent with the entity's plans and expectations
- Logical in the context of the forecast or projection taken as a whole

Assumptions that have no material impact on the forecast or projection need not be specifically evaluated, but the aggregate impact of individually insignificant assumptions must be considered in determining appropriateness.

Benchmarking Assumptions

All valuation methods under the income approach, whether based on an income capitalization or cash flows discounting method, involve some use of a benefit statement or prospective financial information. The benefit stream relates to financial parameters such as revenues; earnings before interest, taxes, depreciation, and amortization (EBITDA); net income; or cash flow, whose estimates are critical to the reliability of the resulting conclusions. In particular, they are required in the application of a sales comparison method, as valuation multiples are applied to prospective as well as to historical financial figures.

There is a link between the basis under which the prospective financial information is prepared and how an appropriate discount rate is determined. In the traditional DCF method, a single most likely forecast of cash flows is made and all risks attaching to both the cash flows and the business are reflected in the discount rate. Under the expected cash flow method, a number of expected cash flows and their probabilities are projected; hence possible variations in the cash flows do not need to be captured in the discount rate.

Properly document the sources of all assumptions used, especially in respect to revenues. Reflect the sales anticipated in the market generally and the entity's expected share, taking into account any available studies relating to the firm's products, services, or technologies.

Other means of benchmarking techniques are trends and patterns developed from its operating history (life cycles of prior generations of products), rates of change in average selling prices and such, and comparing projected operating margins and expense ratios with past relationships reflecting anticipated variations due to market expectations.

Growth rates after the explicit forecast period must be appropriate to the assets' expected lives, as well as the industry and economies involved, together with the markets' outlooks. For businesses, an infinite life is often assumed. For a large corporation, this normally is reasonable; for a small firm, however, no more than 20 years is suggested. The expected long-term growth should not exceed the long-term average growth rate projected by others for the products, industries, and country or countries in which the entity operates, or for the market in which the asset is used, unless a higher rate can be justified. Benchmark all assumptions from as many different sources as possible to assess their appropriateness.

Synergies

In a business combination, the assumptions should take into account not only the various known and possible costs and projected amounts and timings of anticipated synergies. Differentiate those that market participants (normally financial buyers) can achieve by introducing industry best practices from those obtainable only by the specific acquirer (usually a strategic purchaser). There are two major forms of synergies: cost reductions that can often be realized relatively quickly and revenue enhancements that result from strategic factors that can take a substantial time to obtain. Synergies take longer to achieve than expected and usually involve unforeseen costs. Those expected by the acquirer can be incorporated in the cash flow forecasts used for a purchase price allocation (Chapter 13). However, only those obtainable by a market participant may be applied in the GAAP goodwill impairment tests (Chapter 14).

 ## BELIEVABLE AND LIKELY CONCLUSIONS

To confirm the believability of the reported conclusions of a financial forecast or projection, it is essential to examine the procedures adopted by considering the five traditional questions: Who? Why? How? Where? When? A useful sixth is: What happened before? Focus on the key assumptions, which are not always self-evident. They may be implicit in the model rather than being explicitly disclosed. Concentrate on the most important numbers or those with the greatest risks, not just the largest. As set out earlier, confirming the reasonableness of the assumptions adopted is an art, not a science, requiring:

- Industry knowledge
- Experience
- Understanding why the transaction takes place
- Maintaining a healthy dose of skepticism
- Comprehending what management expects to achieve

All financial projections used for fair value are subject to review by an auditor. Since they involve uncertainties and subjectivities, the auditor will assess the degree to which the conclusions could be misstated, in particular:

- The number, significance, and complexity of the assumptions
- Evidence to support them and their degree of subjectivity
- To what extent they depend on the outcome of future events
- The availability of objective data to support them
- The projected period

 ## QUALITY OF EARNINGS

There is a real difference in the quality of earnings that are reported by different types of companies. If you looked at the financial statements of Enron Corporation in the late 1990s and into 2000, to mention a flagrant example, most reported income was unrealized, related to mark-to-market or fair value changes. It doesn't mean that those are not interesting pieces of information—indeed they are—but they are not realized profits. In projecting what is to come, be aware of the distinction between things and actions that generate cash flows and those that do not.

Any income statement today, under GAAP or IFRS, is a hybrid including numbers for both realized and unrealized events. At a glance, it is very difficult for the average investor or creditor, and even for analysts, to understand what portion of the reported income has been realized. The same is true on the balance sheet. A significant portion of the numbers shown on Enron's balance sheet were based on estimated market prices, many related to contracts that ran up to 20 years into the future. A lot can happen in such a period, as shown by events from 1991 to 2010.

In making cash flow projections, essential to DCF models, it is essential to pull past income statements apart, and present very clearly only the expected transactions that generate cash. An open contract can create profits (or losses) but cannot generate cash flows, which is all that matters to investors or creditors.

 CONCLUSION

This chapter has looked at financial projections, which underlie most valuations from the viewpoint of the user as critic. While it set out the major problem areas, it should not be looked on as a cookbook for preparing such a document. Those are best created through well-established models such as those by ValueSource.

CHAPTER SIX

The Market Approach to Fair Value

In the short run the market is a voting machine; in the long run it is a weighing machine.

—Benjamin Graham (1894–1976), American economist and investor

HAPTER 3, "FAIR VALUE FRAMEWORK," briefly mentioned the three accepted valuation approaches and the need, if all are not applied, to explain the reason. This and the next two chapters deal with their positions in the fair value hierarchy and the various methods used to implement them. It is important that managers, who are ultimately responsible for fair values, understand the strengths and weaknesses of each valuation approach. First we discuss the market approach; as fair value concerns itself with market participants, quoted prices in active markets (Level 1 inputs) are the best basis for its measurement. They are available for many financial assets, certain real estate, selected commodities (such as oil or copper), and some forms of plant & equipment (for example, cars or trucks).

NATURE OF MARKETS

Activity in markets, which have buyers as well as sellers, acts as a form of price discovery. There will always be a tendency to movement as buyers' demands for lower prices conflict with sellers' needs to maintain profit margins. The effect is most obvious with perishables, when at the end of Saturday shopping, unsold items are marked down—some revenue today is better than the chance of nothing, from spoiled goods, on Monday.

In free (unregulated) active markets, buyers and sellers come together to exchange goods or services for cash. In other words, they discover an amount that both parties find satisfactory. Low prices are an incentive for greater demand, which then drives them higher. High prices increase competitors (supply), pushing them lower.

Markets can be very unstable; for example, during the week of May 1 to 7, 2011, the price of silver dropped 30% from a high of $47.32 an ounce on Monday to a low of $33.17 on Friday! Over a longer term the effect can be devastating. The U.S. commercial real estate market peaked in 2007; as shown in Figure 6.1 from the *Elliott Wave Theorist*, by the end of 2009 it had given up about 90% of the previous gain from 2001 to the 2007 top.

For investors, the decade from 2000 to 2009 was the most interesting time since I first became involved with stock and commodity markets in 1955. In many cases, what had been active trading markets in (supposedly) AAA-rated securities simply disappeared, as suddenly nobody was sufficiently certain of their quality or that of the underlying items to buy; the only bids were merely indicative ("This is what I might pay if I were really interested"). At those levels, sellers said, "No way," resulting in limited trading. Huge blocks that were previously easily valued with Level 1 inputs suddenly changed to Level 3 conclusions, being marked to models rather than to markets.

In the past 25 years, many parts of the world economy have suffered bubbles. One of the best known was the Japanese real estate and stock market boom that peaked in 1987. At that time, the land around the Imperial Palace in Tokyo was reputed to be worth more than the whole state of California; the boom's collapse led to two lost economic decades for the country.

Of more recent note were the dot-com episode in the United States and a few other stock markets (1995–2000) and the "home ATM" U.S. residential real estate quagmire (2005–2011), when so-called liar loans in many cases became the subprime standard. The mortgage market collapse led to the demise of two of the five great Wall Street investment banks—Bear Stearns and Lehman

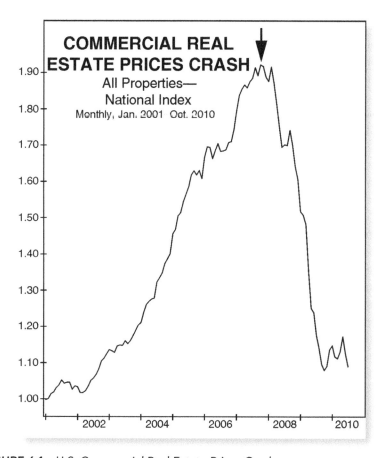

FIGURE 6.1 U.S. Commercial Real Estate Prices Crash

Source: © October 2010 Elliott Wave International (www.elliottwave.com). Data courtesy http://web.mit.edu/cre/research/credl/rca.html.

Brothers—and the forced sale of a third, Merrill Lynch. Lehman failed after 158 years of superb service; when I worked there in the early 1960s, it was an enjoyable experience to be part of an honest creator of wealth for clients, partners, and staff.

Another bubble is still underway—the Asian-driven commodity run-up that accelerated in 2010. According to GMO LLC, a Boston money manager, as reported in the *Economist*, an equally weighted index of 33 commodities fell 70% in real terms during the twentieth century between 1901 and 2000 and regained all of that from 2001 to 2010.

Even with all of those excesses, it is highly desirable, especially for growth companies, to apply some method under the market approach rather than relying completely on those methods under the income approach that are founded solely on investment criteria.

 ## CLASSIFYING ASSETS

Before discussing how assets are valued, it is important to consider how they are classified. For over 100 years, to achieve certainty, accountants recorded them at historical cost, segregated into four categories by liquidity:

1. *Current:* Receivables, inventory, prepaid expenses, and other items expected to be turned into cash within 12 months
2. *Capital:* Property, plant & equipment (PP&E), which contribute to operations for longer than the next 12 months; their costs are recovered by regular depreciation charges to income over their useful lives
3. *Deferred:* Costs incurred during a specific period that create future benefits and are expensed at those relevant times
4. *Intangible:* The costs of purchased items, mainly goodwill, that contribute to future profits and are amortized over their economic lives

In the twenty-first century, GAAP and IFRS have moved toward recording assets in categories that reflect their intrinsic characteristics:

- *Financial:* Cash, investments, loans and advances, prepaid assets, accounts receivable, and other financial instruments
- *Physical:* Inventories and PP&E (owned or held under capital leases), including computer hardware and purchased software
- *Intangible:* All items that meet the Financial Accounting Standards Board's (FASB) or the International Accounting Standards Board's (IASB) legal or separable criteria, some of which may have been previously recorded in deferred costs or goodwill, including:
    - Copyrights—created software, website designs, and the like
    - Delivery channels—distributors, wholesalers, retailers, customer lists
    - Know-how—core technologies, processes, research and development (R&D) projects, trade secrets
    - Licenses and permits—TV/radio, transportation, and so on
    - Operating leases—capital leases are physical assets

- Patents—monopolies of product or processes for a certain period
- Systems—covering leased and copyrighted licensed software for managing, planning, accounting, production, supply chain, environmental, quality control
- Trademarks—brands and products
- *Goodwill:* A residual that includes human capital, which encompasses the education, skills, and collective experience of all employees. Until it was abolished in 2001, the United States and some other jurisdictions had an intangible asset known as "assembled workforce." Another important part of goodwill is future opportunities, projects that are often effectively separable and possibly represent a significant portion of an entity's value.

Application

There are three principal methods for applying the market approach:

1. Recent comparable transactions in the same or similar assets
2. Parameters obtained from guideline entities in the same or similar industries
3. Reported royalty rates for licensing the same type of asset in similar industries

Each method is based on recorded transactions, adjusted for differences in location and other characteristics.

Asset Transactions

When dealing with individual assets or groups of assets that may be sold, leased, or licensed, the following factors are helpful in selecting, comparing, and analyzing transaction data:

- The specific legal rights of ownership conveyed
- Financing terms or other payment arrangements
- Economic and market conditions at the transaction date
- The industry in which the asset exists or will be used
- Physical, functional, technological, and economic characteristics involved
- Other related items included, such as a sale bundled with physical items (for example, the sale of aged whiskey inventories with the brand name and recipe)

The final steps in applying any method under the market approach are to summarize the empirical data for consistency, review the analyses, assess the strengths and weaknesses of each reported transaction as a comparable, and make an overall selection from the data.

COMPARABLE TRANSACTIONS

The comparable transactions method is adopted for items with a significant volume of sale, lease, or licensing transactions in a particular area. Assets commonly covered include shares, bonds, or derivatives (when quoted in an active market); real estate (all residential and much industrial and commercial); standard industrial and mining machinery and equipment (computers, air compressors, tools, cars, trucks, etc.); as well as software, technologies, trademarks, and similar licensed items. Normally adjustments are applied relating to market trends, size, age, and condition.

Valuing Individual Assets

The process of valuing an individual asset under the market approach has four steps:

1. Review available databases for useful information such as sale, lease, or license transactions or listings, as well as offers to purchase and leases or licenses of comparable assets or businesses. Comparability is based on type of asset, its use, the industry in which it operates, date of creation, and remaining useful life.
2. Confirm that the data is accurate and the transactions are at arm's length. This may generate additional information about current market conditions.
3. Select a relevant measure of comparison such as revenue multiples, price to earnings ratio, royalty rate, or dollars per unit, and develop a parallel analysis for all pertinent choices.
4. Compare reported sales, leases, or licenses using the selected measure. If necessary, appropriately adjust each transaction to reflect the fair value of the asset, entity, reporting unit, or cash-generating unit.

Adjustments

At this point, a reader may want to return to Chapter 3, where observable and unobservable inputs are discussed under Stage 5 of the fair value framework. When applying data from comparable transactions, a user must understand that when any adjustment whatsoever (even the most insignificant) is made to a Level 1 input, it becomes Level 2. If the adjustments, as is common with real estate comparables, contain significant subjective (unobservable) factors, the input may now well become Level 3, with a lesser degree of confidence and requiring additional disclosures.

Examples of such adjustments are for size (the valuation multiple is dollars per acre of land or square foot of usable space) or time delays (one sale was 6 months ago, another 14 months earlier), both of which are objective, but also for quality (the subject is better or worse than the comparable), which is mainly subjective.

Caution

In looking at comparable transactions and guideline entities, especially when relying on a database rather than original documents, little weight should be placed on transactions:

- Between related parties
- That took place under duress or were forced
- That had a different unit of account from the asset for which fair value is being determined
- That were in a market in which the entity would not normally deal

Marketability

For many organizations, financial assets are reported at fair value (commonly marked-to-market quotations). Under normal circumstances this is fine; however, after 2008, when many markets became inactive, quotations had to be replaced by so-called marked-to-model methods, usually involving Level 3 inputs. This often had a significant impact, as the revised values not only reflected alterations in the assets' credit standing relating to the borrowers' ability to make interest and principal payments as they came due, but also significant structural (noncredit) factors such as a discount for lack of marketability (DLOM), the latter frequently being the majority of the changes. If these are not separately stated, a user should try to carefully differentiate them.

When utilizing a method under the market approach to value a firm, it is essential that:

- The business is mature and well established
- Data on similar, actively traded entities is accessible (guideline entities technique)
- Recent transactions for similar companies (comparable transaction technique) are available

In most countries, the guideline entities technique is more prevalent, as sufficient information is not often available to apply the comparable transaction technique. However, if there is enough data to express the price in dollars per unit of output (barrel, ton, area, or revenue), it may corroborate a value conclusion, or at least supply an indication of reasonableness.

 GUIDELINE ENTITIES

Identifying comparable transactions or guideline entities requires judgment, taking into account the nature of the business, products or services, diversity of markets and geography involved, financial performance, and potential risks. There are over 40,000 firms in the world with publicly traded securities. From this universe it is normally possible to find at least one entity (and hopefully several) in the same or a related industry that is sufficiently similar that its share price parameters (price/earnings, price/sales, price/book value, business enterprise value/EBITDA, etc.) are reasonably applicable to the subject. In applying this method, those measurements for each guideline are then weighted.

Selection Process

The selection process involves the following procedures:

- Research the industry and the subject entity.
- Analyze historical financial performance of the subject.
- Adjust for nonrecurring items.
- Search databases to identify potential comparable entities or guideline transactions.
- Establish final selection based on weighing relevant comparability.
- Determine any adjustment to the comparables or guidelines.
- Choose and calculate appropriate valuation multiples.
- Establish the magnitude of any acquisition premium.

Sources of Company Information

Much of the search for guideline transactions and comparable entities can be undertaken on the Internet, where a great deal of information, both financial and operational, is available concerning firms issuing publicly traded securities.

Once a ticker symbol is obtained (an easy source is Yahoo Finance's Symbol Lookup), material on most U.S. and many foreign traded entities is available at:

- *BigCharts* (http://bigcharts.marketwatch.com): Graphic displays of up to 10 years of price performance of over 15,000 stocks and indexes in many countries
- *Business.com* (www.business.com): News, research, and contacts for 10,000 public and 44,000 private companies
- *CorporateInformation* (www.corporateinformation.com): U.S. and international company data, including profiles, research studies and reports, and earnings information
- *DailyStocks* (www.dailystocks.com): Extensive company information, including quotes, profiles, charts, news, SEC filings, and articles
- *Aswath Damodaran Online* (www.stern.nyu.edu/~adamodar): An excellent source for financial technicians
- *EDGAR* (www.sec.gov): SEC website with complete filings from all registrants; see www.sec.gov/edgar/searchedgar/webusers.htm for historical data from 1994 to 2011
- *Hoover's* (www.hoovers.com): A respected service providing timely and detailed information on over 50,000 public and private mainly U.S. companies
- *IndustryWatch* (www.industrywatch.com): High-level information similar to Hoover's but organized differently
- *OneSource* (www.onesource.com): A comprehensive subscription service that can be searched by North American Industry Classification System (NAICS) code to identify competitors
- *Reuters:* (www.reuters.com): A source of financial information on over 10,000 public companies
- *Yahoo Finance:* (http://finance.yahoo.com): Comprehensive data on public companies from Reuters, PR Newswire, Businesswire, and Market Guide, with specific sites for many countries

Weighting Guidelines or Comparables

Table 6.1 shows one means of weighting guideline transactions of comparable publicly traded entities. Across the top are the selected measures of comparability, in this case six, followed by their percentage significance. The subsequent four lines rank each selected comparable's similarity to the subject, from 1 (low resemblance) to 5 (high resemblance); those index numbers are then multiplied

TABLE 6.1 Example of Guideline Weighting

Guideline	Business	Location	Leverage Measures	Profit Measures	Return on Equity	Growth	Company Weightings
Significance	25%	15%	10%	15%	15%	20%	
Company A	5	2	2	3	3	4	22%
Company B	5	1	4	4	4	2	22%
Company C	4	5	3	5	5	5	30%
Company D	5	5	4	4	4	2	26%

by the relevant significance and totaled to give the company's weighting for the appropriate valuation measures.

Industry Background

An important part of selecting guidelines is learning about the industry:

- What are the revenue trends and areas of growth?
- How do the entities rank by market share?
- Which products and services are in greatest demand?
- When will new technologies have any effect?

This industry information is also important when valuing individual, especially intangible, assets. Obviously, a more accurate conclusion is obtained when the user has a good understanding of the industry and its context, as well as the asset and the entity. Answers to the previous questions can often be found at:

- *CorporateInformation* (www.corporateinformation.com): Links to industry resources in more than 30 sectors
- *BNET* (http://findarticles.com) *and MagPortal* (www.magportal.com): Sites that allow searches of over 300 periodicals, journals, and newswires
- *Fuld & Company* (www.fuld.com) *and Industry Research Desk* (www.virtu-alpet.com/industry): Links to U.S. and international industry home pages in over 30 areas
- *Hoover's Industry Overviews* (http://www.hoovers.com/hooversdirec-tories/industryIndex-1.html): Detailed surveys of and news articles on 28 sectors

- *Morningstar* (Morningstar.com): Valuation information for many countries
- *ValuationResources.com* (http://valuationresources.com): Source of useful material such as company, industry, and economic data

Control Premiums

The quoted market price of an individual share (the usual unit of account) multiplied by the number of shares outstanding gives the market capitalization of an entity, such as a reporting or cash-generating unit, with publicly traded equity; normally, this does not represent the fair value of the particular firm as a whole. Acquirers are usually willing to pay a premium for shares representing a controlling interest over the amount an investor would pay for the same number of shares reflecting a minority position, as such a buyer gains the advantage of synergies and other benefits through control. Consequently, the fair value of the collection of assets and liabilities that make up a controlled entity is different from (likely greater than) that of the total of the market capitalizations of its individual securities. Numerous organizations, such as Mergerstat, collect information regarding control premiums in merger transactions in the United States and some other countries; a common level is 30%.

 GUIDELINE ENTITIES EXAMPLE

The objective is to determine the fair value of all the shares of privately owned Alpha Manufacturing Company by the market approach. Management is aware of eight publicly traded companies in the same industry, some with higher and some with lower reported sales than Alpha. A significant factor affecting Alpha is its shutdown of two money-losing plants at the end of the previous fiscal year, their revenues representing about 18% of its previous total.

With guideline entities, the most commonly adopted and most satisfactory (according to academic research) valuation multiple is business enterprise value (BEV) divided by OPEBITDA. BEV is defined as the total enterprise value (the sum of all interest-bearing debt, preferred shares, and common equity market capitalization; TEV) less any excess cash or redundant assets not involved directly in the business. OPEBITDA is operating earnings before interest, taxes, depreciation, and amortization (EBITDA) for the latest 12 months (LTM). As shown in Table 6.2, three of the eight guideline entities in this example had OPEBITDA multiples that were either extreme or negative for the LTM; therefore, management also considered two other related multiples; the first was

TABLE 6.2   Guideline Valuation Multiples

Guideline	Valuation Multiples		
	Sales	OPEBITDA	OPEBITRAD
A	1.30	8.82	4.36
B	0.12	2.43	0.74
C	2.71	513.61	12.59
D	2.70	11.41	6.31
E	3.45	28.88	5.36
F	0.55	(4.69)	2.34
G	0.49	9,759	2.57
H	0.75	8.30	2.97
Mean	1.51	1,291	4.65
Median	1.03	10.12	3.67

BEV/sales and the second was BEV/operating earnings before interest, taxes, R&D, amortization, and depreciation (OPEBITRAD), which treats R&D as a capital rather than an operating expenditure.

Application of Value Multiples

As the means and the medians of the selected valuation multiples varied significantly, rather than weighting each guideline individually, management decided to adopt weighted averages of the medians (80%) and means (20%). Based on that procedure, the value multiples shown in Table 6.3 were developed after applying both a 30% control premium (reflecting a 23% minority discount) and a 43% DLOM based on U.S. pre–initial public offering (IPO) studies, as the subject, Alpha, is privately owned.

TABLE 6.3   Adjustments to Value Multiples

Guideline	Valuation Multiples		
	Sales	OPEBITDA	OPEBITRAD
Weighted average multiples	1.122	26.628	3.863
Control premium: 30%	0.337	7.988	1.159
DLOM: 43%	(0.482)	(11.450)	(1.661)
Selected multiple	0.976	23.166	3.361

TABLE 6.4 Calculation for Alpha's BEV ($ thousands)

	Sales	OPEBITDA	OPEBITRAD	Average
Alpha actual	195,095	944	24,509	
Indicated BEV	190,413	21,864	82,374	98,217
Alpha forecast	160,503	2,865	20,656	
Indicated BEV	156,651	66,375	69,424	97,483

Fair Value

Table 6.4 shows the indicated BEV of Alpha, based on the latest actual results and a projection for the next year using market participants', rather than management's assumptions.

The average results for each year are within ±0.5% of their midpoint, even though the dispersion of the underlying figures is very wide. Therefore management considered it reasonable to select the midpoint of $97,850,000 as the BEV. The figure for the estimated fair value for Alpha's equity is $87,750,000, made up as shown in Table 6.5.

Actual EBITDA Multiples

Table 6.6, based on information from Fitch Ratings and other sources, sets out as a guide to possible multiples the historical (2001–2010) LTM TEV/EBITDA ratios for U.S. industrial sectors, representing 90% of the country's commercial economy.

TABLE 6.5 Calculation of Alpha's Equity Value ($ thousands)

BEV	97,850
Excess cash and marketable securities	4,093
Term bank loans	(6,690)
Note payable to supplier	(2,800)
Loans from affiliate	(4,824)
Value of equity	87,629
Rounded	87,750

TABLE 6.6 U.S. Enterprise Values 2001–2010 (LTM EBITDA Multiples)

	Low	High	Average	Recent	Volatility	Fitch Recovery	Portion of Recent
Aerospace & defense	6.5	11.9	9.3	10.5	183%	7.0	67%
Auto & related	5.2	8.5	7.1	7.5	163%	4.8	64%
Chemicals	6.4	11.3	8.4	7.7	177%	5.1	66%
Consumer (durable & nondurable)	7.1	10.7	8.5	8.8	151%	10.9	124%
Diversified services	5.2	11.2	9.2	10.0	215%	n/a	n/a
Energy	4.5	9.9	7.6	9.3	220%	5.6	60%
Food, beverage, tobacco, & restaurants	6.2	10.6	8.0	7.2	171%	7.5	104%
Gaming, lodging, & leisure	7.7	11.2	9.4	9.2	145%	7.2	78%
Health care	7.0	11.5	9.5	9.1	164%	7.0	77%
Homebuilding, material, & construction	6.3	24.8	11.1	15.2	394%	n/a	n/a
Manufacturing & capital goods	5.6	11.5	8.7	11.5	205%	4.8	42%
Media & entertainment	6.1	13.0	10.1	7.3	213%	5.5	75%
Natural resources	5.9	10.3	8.4	9.2	175%	7.0	76%
Retail	5.7	8.3	7.1	7.0	146%	6.6	94%
Technology	6.8	14.3	10.2	9.9	210%	5.4	55%
Telecommunications & cable	7.2	21.6	13.0	11.2	300%	7.3	65%
Transportation	7.0	12.8	9.6	8.6	183%	3.7	43%
Utilities	6.4	11.8	8.8	7.7	184%	5.8	75%

 ## LICENSED ASSET EXAMPLE

For many assets, there is no effective market in which they are bought or sold but a significant one in which they are licensed or rented. A major set of valuation methods under the market approach is based on the concept that the value of an asset is the amount an entity not owning it would pay for a right of use. Often called the relief-from-royalty method, it commonly applies to intangible assets or to items such as office space that are normally licensed or leased, rather than owned. It capitalizes, or discounts, the estimated amounts of royalties or rents the owner saves by not having to pay others for its use.

The royalty rate chosen is based on analyses of empirical, market-derived, reported royalty terms for comparable items, using the databases that summarize licensing and leasing transactions for many types of assets reported to various regulators. The first step in applying this method is to project revenues over the asset's expected remaining economic life. A market-derived royalty rate is then applied to determine the estimated savings. Depending on circumstances, a pre- or after-tax amount is calculated for each year and discounted to a present value (PV), in a manner similar to the discounted cash flow method (see Chapter 8).

Alpha has some propriety technology to be valued for an impairment test at December 31, 2010; it comprises two patents, some copyrighted software, and considerable know-how protected as trade secrets, a form of intellectual property. To obtain an appropriate rate, management searches databases for comparable licenses in the applicable NAICS codes. The search results in eight currently in-force agreements for the use of technology by similar firms, with the characteristics shown in Table 6.7.

Excluding the 30% rate that applied solely to specialized software, the mean is 6.2% and the median 5.0%; the latter was selected and applied to the projected revenues from both the existing and the in-development new products, together with their planned replacements for another generation, in total,

TABLE 6.7 Comparable Royalty Rate

Royalty Rate (%)	Number	
1.0	2	Mean 12.1%
5.0	2	Median 8.5%
12.0	1	Standard deviation 11.8%
13.0	1	
30.1	2	
	8	

TABLE 6.8 Value of Alpha Technology ($ thousands)

Year	Revenues	Growth	Royalty (5.0%)	PV Factor	Present Value (29%)
2011	6,764		338	0.8734	295
2012	7,170	6.0%	359	0.6770	243
2013	7,887	10.0%	394	0.5248	207
2014	8,518	8.0%	426	0.4068	173
2015	9,029	6.0%	451	0.3154	142
2016	9,481	5.0%	474	0.2445	116
2017	9,860	4.0%	493	0.1895	93
					1,270

covering the remaining seven-year life of the more recent patent; after that, some of the technologies will be in the public domain.

Table 6.8 sets out anticipated revenues for 2009 to 2013 given to the board of directors in a management forecast, which management believes would be acceptable to a market participant, plus projections for subsequent years using declining growth rates. Applying a pretax discount rate of 29% based on venture capitalists' (market participants') views, the method gives a value of $1.27 million for Alpha's technology.

 CONCLUSION

A method under the market approach that involves information from actual transactions should be applied in estimating fair value, as, by definition, they are the amounts market participants would pay. However, in many cases, there is insufficient data and therefore another approach is more likely to result in a better-substantiated conclusion.

CHAPTER SEVEN

The Cost Approach to Fair Value

Valuation is an art, not an exact science. Mathematical certainty is not demanded, nor indeed is it possible.

—*Viscount Simon (1873–1954), British jurist*

THE COST OF ANY PARTICULAR ASSET does not normally represent its fair value. But in practice, replacement cost of an asset adjusted for time to use establishes a ceiling for its fair value, as it is the maximum amount a prudent investor will pay. There may be exceptions for unique items such as antiques, but fair value is intended to overrule sentiment and emotion. Hence the cost approach is most useful as a sanity check.

 ## CURRENT REPLACEMENT COST

Obtaining a current replacement cost for an existing item is done by first determining the expenditure needed to re-create its functionality as new using the latest technologies, then deducting amounts for each of four factors: functional

deterioration, technical obsolescence, physical decline, and economic deprivation. None, either individually or in total, will be the same as the familiar accounting depreciation used to amortize the capitalized costs of an asset over its useful
life. If the actual item is less useful than an ideal replacement, the amount must be
lowered. Replacement cost is not the same as duplication (sometimes called reproduction) cost, which refers to re-creating an identical asset. Nor is it the same as
creation cost that adjusts the original expenditures for changes in price levels.

Real Estate

The current replacement cost method is particularly important for real estate,
often a significant component of a reporting unit or cash-generating unit.
Under GAAP, the fair value of real estate is split between land and buildings. IFRS requires further subdivision into major components, which may
have different remaining useful lives (RULs). It is usually relatively easy to
gauge the contribution of the land based on sales data in the area. Pertinent
information concerning a building's various elements can be obtained from
engineering cost manuals and confirmed by local contractors, real estate
agents, and taxing authorities; fair value is then allocated pro rata. Table 7.1
demonstrates the process and the allocations under both Generally Accepted
Accounting Principles (GAAP) and International Financial Reporting Standards (IFRS) of the fair value of an office building, obtained by a market
approach method.

TABLE 7.1 Sample Real Estate Fair Value Allocation ($ thousands)

	Market Approach	Cost Approach		Allocated Fair Values GAAP	Allocated Fair Values IFRS
Land	11,600	33.4%		11,369	11,369
Building				22,631	
Electrical	5,260	15.2%			5,155
Elevator	2,620	7.6%			2,568
HVAC	5,120	14.8%			5,018
Mechanical	1,640	4.7%			1,607
Structure	7,400	21.3%			7,253
Roof	—	1,050	3.0%	—	1,029
	34,000	34,690	100.0%	34,000	34,000

Inventories, Plant & Equipment

To establish amounts for other physical assets such as inventories or plant & equipment, it is necessary to differentiate between assets that are generally available and those that are custom-built. For generally available items, replacement cost is the price in the secondhand market of physically and functionally similar used items, of comparable capacity and utility, plus setup costs and installed computer software. Where a specific unit is too outdated for any comparison, the replacement cost of a similar but newer product may be used, less provisions for condition, age, and obsolescence.

Custom-built assets, specifically designed for one particular purpose, have limited alternative applications; for them, replacement cost is the total of the estimated expenditures necessary to create and put into position reasonably similar equipment, giving consideration to condition, age, productive capacity, and obsolescence.

DEDUCTIONS

The replacement cost method requires estimating the amounts to be deducted for each of four factors: functional deterioration, technical obsolescence, physical decline, and economic deprivation.

1. *Functional deterioration:* The loss in value resulting from a relative inability of the asset to fulfill its intended purpose. For example, a telephone system might have to add new features; therefore, the existing equipment's ability to satisfy users' requirements is lessened, even though the installation remains in first-class condition.
2. *Technological obsolescence:* The loss in value resulting from the introduction of a new process that significantly lowers operating expenses or improves quality. For example, many traditional printing presses that had been useful for more than half a century were made immediately obsolete by new equipment using direct digital inputs.
3. *Physical decline:* The loss in value from the passage of time. Older equipment, even well maintained and retaining full functionality, has a reduced value due to the difficulty of finding spare parts and trained technicians. For example, DC-3 aircraft (Dakotas) are still flying in some parts of the world over 75 years after they were introduced in 1935, because sufficient numbers were built to allow cannibalization.

4. *Economic deprivation:* The loss in value due to external influences such as a major drop-off in a market. In spite of temporary fashion blips and seasonal upsurges, demand for women's and men's hats virtually disappeared during the 1960s, resulting in a drastic reduction in the value of the assets used to make them.

The remainder of this section may not interest everyone, as it deals with judging the amounts to be deducted for each factor. However, as adjusted replacement cost establishes the highest amount a prudent investor will pay, calculating such deductions is important. Partially based on engineering studies, the amount for each factor is also dependent on the valuator's experience and the ability to find appropriate data. The larger the amount for a factor, the higher the uncertainties involved.

Functional Deterioration

There can be many forms of functional deterioration, making it difficult to separately quantify the effect of each. The most common causes are regulatory events or changes in market expectations of future demand; both contribute to the level and rate of functional deterioration and directly or indirectly lower the usefulness of the asset. The combined effect is reflected in a reduction in its utilization relative to that of newer and more functional items.

Many practitioners use comparison methods under the market approach to assess this factor, especially for property, plant & equipment, because functional deterioration tends to be reflected in market prices. While this has merit, it does not fully account for the effect that future changes may have on current economic lives and values. Using a market-based method inherently but incorrectly assumes that the rate of functional deterioration realized to date will remain constant in the future; in fact, it is likely to increase over time. Such methods tend to overstate an asset's economic life and its fair value. It is preferable to establish the amounts required to remedy the current deterioration and to estimate those that will be needed in the future. Some valuators treat technological obsolescence as part of functional deterioration, but in my view they are very different.

Technological Obsolescence

Most entities, in a process known as technology substitution, replace existing equipment with items using new technologies to improve efficiency—lower operating or capital costs per unit of output, greater capacity in the same physical space, better quality, and the like. This process, which can be measured and plotted over time, inevitably demonstrates an S-curve. Although the pattern had been known for years, it was only in 1971 that J. C. Fisher and R. H. Pry, of General Electric, defined it in their book *A Simple Substitution Model of Technological Change, Technological Forecasting and Social Change*.

The Fisher-Pry S-curve has proven to be highly accurate in predicting the pace of technology substitution and the resulting technological obsolescence. By 1986, according to R. C. Lenz and L. K. Vanston in *Comparisons of Technology Substitutions in Telecommunications and Other Industries*, over 200 such substitutions in the United States, covering industries ranging from chemicals to aviation, had been identified as reasonable fits. In each case, the form of the S-curve allowed it to be projected into the future and used to directly determine the deduction.

Documenting Obsolescence

Industries seem to constantly find new uses for computers; examples are enhanced financial or operational control and planning systems, as well as developing new technologies and processes. While the value of a firm is enhanced by such activities, they tend to require constant replacement of the relevant hardware. Some entities face capacity constraints or cannot afford such additional investments; they must keep their existing equipment in service for longer than management would like, even though it clearly shows the effects of technological obsolescence.

To document this situation:

- Compare the cost, speed, and efficiency of all technology-oriented assets with those of the newest, most efficient alternatives available.
- Compile market data such as list prices, useful lives, and current trade-in amounts.
- Follow economic trends, and gather reports on the industry and on competitors' practices.
- Collect plant-level costs to identify the effect on profitability of retaining existing assets.
- Estimate the cost to refurbish and de-bottleneck plants not functioning at capacity.
- Ask plant engineers and equipment operators about the need to replace particular items.

Physical Decline

Physical decline is the loss in value of an asset due to usage, wear and tear, exposure to the elements, age, accidental loss or destruction, or the difficulty of finding spare parts and trained technicians. It has similarities to traditional accounting depreciation showing decrease in value over time from original cost to scrap. As it reflects physical changes, the amounts tend to be higher in the early years and lower in later periods.

Economic Deprivation

Economic deprivation relates to declines in value resulting from external influences. This, in essence, is everything not reflected in the other three factors. Although it takes a variety of forms, it is essential to document its impact at annual rates so that all the factors may be easily combined. Unlike physical decline, which tends to uniformly apply to assets of a particular vintage (purchased in the same year), economic deprivation generally affects all similar items regardless of their age.

For example, a local telephone supplier expected to lose 30% of its domestic customers from 2004 to 2007. Management's analyses projected a loss of 5% in the first year, 12% of those remaining in each of the next two, and a final 5% in the fourth. After that, it believed that gains from competitors would offset further losses. These projected customer loss percentages represent annual probable economic deprivation in a readily combinable form.

 INTEGRATING THE FACTORS

Integrating the impacts of the various factors is essential in determining the accumulated decrease in value. This is commonly done chronologically, to facilitate valuing the assets on the same basis as they are recorded in the entity's records. It is not simple addition; if in a year, one asset has a probable 10% physical decline, only the remaining 90% will be subject to the 15% anticipated technological obsolescence. Therefore, at the end of the period, 76.5% [90% × (1 − 15%)] is likely to be in service and the net probable decrease is 23.5% (1 − 76.5%) rather than 25% (10% + 15%).

Table 7.2 gives projected annual impact rates for each of the four factors and their combined effect for an asset class with a 20-year physical life and a 7.5% salvage value. The average physical life (50% of the value) is 7.6 years,

TABLE 7.2 Annual Probabilities for a Year's Asset Class

Year	Functional Deterioration	Technological Obsolescence	Physical Decline	Economic Deprivation	Net Decrease	Surviving Value 100%	Subtotal C + D = H	Subtotal H + B = 1	Physical Value	Functional Value
1 1999	0.0%	1.3%	4.0%	0.0	5.2	94.8%	5.2%	5.2%	96.0%	100.0%
2 2000	0.0%	2.0%	8.0%	0.0	9.8	85.4%	9.8%	9.8%	88.3%	100.0%
3 2001	0.0%	2.9%	8.5%	5.0	15.6	72.1%	11.2%	11.2%	80.8%	100.0%
4 2002	1.0%	4.3%	9.0%	15.0	26.7	52.8%	12.9%	13.8%	73.5%	100.0%
5 2003	2.0%	6.1%	9.5%	15.0	29.2	37.4%	15.0%	16.7%	66.6%	99.0%
6 2004	2.5%	8.6%	10.0%	5.0	23.8	28.5%	17.7%	19.8%	59.9%	97.0%
7 2005	3.0%	11.5%	10.5%	0.0	23.2	21.9%	20.8%	23.2%	53.6%	94.6%
8 2006	3.5%	15.0%	11.0%	0.0	27.0	16.0%	24.4%	27.0%	47.7%	91.8%
9 2007	4.0%	18.6%	11.5%	0.0	30.8	11.1%	28.0%	30.8%	42.2%	88.5%
10 2008	4.5%	22.1%	12.0%	0.0	34.5	7.2%	31.4%	34.5%	37.2%	85.0%
11 2009	5.0%	25.2%	12.5%	0.0	37.8	4.5%	34.6%	37.8%	32.5%	81.2%
12 2010	5.5%	27.7%	13.0%	0.0	40.6	2.7%	37.1%	40.6%	28.3%	77.1%
13 2011	6.0%	27.7%	13.5%	0.0	41.2	1.6%	37.5%	41.2%	24.5%	72.9%
14 2012	6.5%	27.7%	14.0%	0.0	41.9	0.9%	37.8%	41.9%	21.0%	68.5%
15 2013	7.0%	27.7%	14.5%	0.0	42.5	0.5%	38.2%	42.5%	18.0%	64.1%
16 2014	7.5%	27.7%	15.0%	0.0	43.2	0.3%	38.5%	43.2%	15.3%	59.6%
17 2015	8.0%	27.7%	15.5%	0.0	43.8	0.2%	38.9%	43.8%	12.9%	55.1%
18 2016	8.5%	27.7%	16.0%	0.0	44.4	0.1%	39.3%	44.4%	10.9%	50.7%
19 2017	9.0%	27.7%	16.5%	0.0	45.1	0.1%	39.6%	45.1%	9.1%	46.4%
20 2018	9.5%	27.7%	17.0%	0.0	45.7	0.0%	40.0%	45.7%	7.5%	42.2%

while on the same basis, the average economic life is 4.2 years (45% less) due to the impact of the other factors.

A separate table is needed for the assets acquired in any particular year—a single vintage; the survivor value for all vintages combined can be plotted to give a visual representation of the total impact on the entity.

RESIDUAL VALUE

All physical items have some value. Discarded equipment may be refurbished and resold, while defective items can be disposed of as scrap. The minimum value of an asset is its net salvage value (NSV)—the proceeds of a sale, less the costs of removal, refurbishment, and so on. This is typically expressed as a percentage of the original cost.

Ultimately, the quality of a valuation by the replacement cost method is only as good as the deductions relating to the four factors. Therefore, values obtained by the cost approach are most appropriate as a ceiling or as a support to results obtained by other approaches; both FASB and IASB acknowledge its usefulness.

USEFUL LIVES

Another way of looking at the four factors is the concept of asset depletion. This is the reduction in future cash flows that are expected over the asset's RUL. For many new assets, the value begins to decrease as soon as they are put to use, and the RUL gradually diminishes. The best-known example is the automobile, whose fair value drops the moment it is driven out of the showroom or off the lot. Regardless of how physical or intangible assets are obtained—acquired in a business combination, purchased as a group or individually—their accounting treatment depends on their estimated RUL to the entity; they should reflect the period over which they will contribute directly or indirectly to cash flows.

An asset's economic or productive life is not identical with its useful life, as management may consider it able to generate cash flows beyond the time the reporting or cash-generating unit anticipates disposing of it. The amortization period would be that of expected ownership, considering any probable residual amount. Some intangible assets, such as noncompetition agreements, contribute only indirectly to future cash flows; in such cases, their amortization should be their legal lives.

Remaining Useful Life Analyses

The RUL of an asset is the period during which it is expected to help, directly or indirectly, generate cash flows for the entity; estimates are usually based on the following factors:

- Anticipated use by the entity
- Expected useful lives of related assets
- Legal or regulatory restrictions
- Effects of obsolescence
- Required maintenance expenditures
- External economic factors
- Uncertain continuity of revenues depending on retaining key employees
- The churn rate of customers
- Mobility of the customer base and employees

The entity's anticipated use of the assets is the most important part of the analyses. If it is less than the physical or legal life, a residual value should be obtained from transactions in an existing market. Legal and regulatory restrictions can provide an indication of the economic lives of certain intangible assets, but their remaining useful lives may be substantially different. In calculating fair values, the RUL is the shortest of the economic, legal, or regulatory periods taking into account all the four factors. The one most likely to have an impact is technological obsolescence. For example, the introduction of the DVD rapidly reduced VCR sales; consequently, the RUL of the related patents declined drastically.

Over time, an asset's ability to perform its original function may deteriorate due to one or more of the four factors. It is therefore necessary to understand the characteristics of physical and intangible assets and their position in the relevant life cycle of the firm, as well as the industry. Maintenance expenditures may also supply information as to an asset's RUL; if they are substantial, a limited life is suggested. When the fair value of an asset is based on discounted cash flows, the period for which they have been projected by management may supply guidance as to their view of the relevant RUL. Indications of a short useful life are projected cash flows based on the expectation of continuous or periodic replacement with similar items, such as acquired customer contracts, or significant costs planned to maintain, renew, enhance, or extend the asset.

Intangible Assets

The RUL of any asset is determined by its ability to produce an economic return that is satisfactory to its owner, given the inherent risks. Once an asset no longer generates this, its economic useful life has come to an end. This is important for intangible assets such as development rights, proprietary technology, copyrights, trademarks, trade names, and advertising materials.

Some intangible assets are directly connected to physical items, so market participants would need both. An example is the link between inventories and brand names—a whiskey distiller must keep sufficient stock to allow proper aging. Another example is a professional athlete's contract, an intangible asset that may lose significant value if the player is injured.

Specific factors relating to the useful lives of intangible assets are:

- *The source.* For those arising from a particular contract, such as licenses, franchises, supply contracts, or permits, the useful life will likely be similar.
- *Relevant legislation.* The RULs for noncompetition agreements, copyrights, trademarks, and trade names are the periods during which they are legally protected.
- *Technological or product life cycles.* As shown in Figure 7.1, life cycles for items such as core technologies must be analyzed to determine the period during which they will be able to perform the intended functions.
- *Rapidly changing technologies.* These assets often have short useful lives, although enhancements may allow other intangibles to function more efficiently (e.g., have a faster processing time or provide a product in a more cost-effective manner).
- *Economic trends.* Changed market conditions could significantly affect supply and demand characteristics of a firm's customers and their value, as well as characteristics of the products or services for which the intangible asset is required.

While the factors just mentioned are the most important, given the material impact that RUL analyses have on the value of an asset, it is imperative to consider all quantitative and qualitative aspects of the particular intangible, especially economic trends, the owner's strategies, regulatory policies, and technological advances.

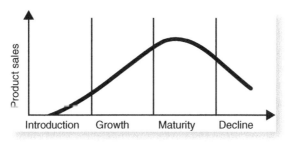

FIGURE 7.1 Example of Product Life Cycle

Source: Anson Marston, Robley Winfrey, and Jean C. Hempstead, *Engineering Valuation and Depreciation* (Ames: Iowa State University Press, 1953).

Survivor Curves

An asset's value changes over time depending on the characteristics of its service life and the anticipated future cash flows it will generate. If the latter are assumed to remain uniform over the various reporting periods, a survivor curve technique (which is beyond the scope of this book) may be used to establish the current value of probable future capabilities available from the asset. Survivor curves are often applied to pools of intangible assets whose values are expected to decrease over time in the normal course of business; examples are customer lists, bank deposits, and advertising campaigns.

The genesis of those curves was management's need, in the early 1900s, to know how long the property, plant & equipment of U.S. railroads would last and when they should be replaced. Based on historical attrition rates, survivor curves may be used to estimate the decay rate of a group of similar physical or intangible items (e.g., computer programs) over time. The same theory, in a slightly modified form, is used by actuaries to estimate human life spans.

Indefinite Lives

Both GAAP and IFRS state that the asset's RUL may be deemed indefinite if analyses of all pertinent factors, including those mentioned earlier, conclude that no legal, regulatory, contractual, competitive, economic, or other factors limit the period; indefinite does not mean indeterminate or infinite. The probability that any asset will become worthless must be considered, even if its precise RUL is unknown.

Some licenses or permits, such as those for broadcasters or hospitals, are initially issued for finite periods, but renewals are usually granted at little or no cost. Some will trade at prices that reflect a life significantly longer than their remaining legal term, indicating that a renewal is expected. For that reason, their lives may also be considered indefinite. For other types of licenses, renewals are not assured and to extend them may incur substantial costs.

Because the useful lives of certain intangible assets depend on renewals and associated costs, FASB decided that their useful lives should reflect a renewal only if there is evidence that it could be obtained without substantial expenditures. Some intangible assets are based on legal rights in perpetuity rather than for a finite term (e.g., water rights). If they are expected to have cash flows associated with them for a long time, they are assumed to have an indefinite RUL.

Entertainment Assets

Movies, television shows, video games, and related assets fall within the scope of a specialized GAAP provision. Those are recorded in accordance with that guidance and amortized by the individual-item-forecast method. In this, the total cash flows expected from a project are estimated, together with all the costs expected to be incurred. The latter are then amortized on the basis of the portion of that cash flow that is received during the period. This provision, which does not contemplate the concept of indefinite life, applies to all kinds of entertainment products, including feature films, television specials and series, animated productions, original soundtrack recordings, music albums, or similar items that are sold, licensed, or exhibited in film, video, and audio, in any format.

Amortization

If an asset has a determinable RUL, the amortization expense should reflect the pattern in which its economic benefits are anticipated to arise. If the relevant pattern cannot be readily determined, the straight-line method is suggested. The residual value for intangibles is generally zero, while physical items have at least their NSV. The RUL of every asset has to be redetermined each time it is tested for impairment under GAAP, which is required at least annually; impairment losses are recognized based on fair values. Physical assets do not decline in value linearly; nor do intangible assets, although they are often amortized on a straight-line basis for accounting purposes. Both tend to exhibit a decay rate, rapid in the early years, then slowing. An example is a customer list that includes initial and latest purchase dates, from which it is possible to project the decline rate and hence its RUL.

If an asset has a finite useful life whose length is not exactly known, it should be amortized over the best estimate of the period. Unless it becomes impaired, an intangible asset should not be written down or off. A reporting or cash-generating unit must examine the pattern of economic benefits expected from each intangible asset before applying the straight-line method. Generally, acquired customer contracts, subject to routine attrition, produce greater cash flows in the early years; this offers reliable evidence that they should be amortized on an accelerated basis.

Occasionally, an intangible asset being amortized is later deemed to have an indefinite life. The best-known example is the cartoon character Mickey Mouse, whose copyright, which was close to expiring, was extended by a change in U.S. law during the 1990s. When such an event occurs, amortization ceases and the intangible should immediately be tested for impairment in the same manner as other assets with indefinite lives. Any resulting loss is recognized in income, not as a change in accounting principles.

VALUING INTANGIBLE ASSETS BY THE COST APPROACH

The remainder of this chapter demonstrates the versatility of the cost approach by showing how fair values can be determined for three different types of intangible assets: the copyright of a safety training DVD, internally developed software systems for operating a firm, and an assembled workforce.

Safety Training DVD

Aria Corporation, a specialist lawn care organization, developed a 30-minute safety training DVD created by a specialized independent producer based on an illness and injury prevention project conducted by a state university. The objective was to reduce job-related injuries among Aria's approximately 1,200 staff and franchise technicians. The material became known for its success in improving operators' efficiency and in lowering workers' compensation claims. At the time it was produced, it was the only vehicle to promoting safety and preventing job-related injuries in the landscaping industry. As a result, Aria's parent, Greensleeves Inc., which did not own all the shares, wanted to adopt it for its other lawn care operations. The purpose of the valuation was to establish a transfer price between the related entities.

Why the Cost Approach?

The cost approach was selected because the DVD:

- Was developed specifically to train lawn care technicians in safety aware-ness and injury prevention. Its intellectual content was derived from the state university's knowledge and experience of safety awareness.
- Represented the only known safety training for lawn care firms; therefore, transactions in comparative copyrights were not available, making the market approach impractical.
- Had no income-producing purpose. The only benefit that could be quanti-fied was the savings in workers' compensation costs.

In addition, all direct, indirect, and opportunity costs related to its creation were readily determinable and traceable.

Replacement Costs

The replacement costs were established from the following calculations:

- Direct overhead- and benefit-related costs of the actual content
- All additional costs related to the production
- Estimates of the intellectual content costs based on the need to reproduce the safety-related knowledge and experience that formed the basis for the DVD, including re-creating data related to all of the following:
  - History of accident claims
  - Experience of several individuals with operating a trimmer
  - Types of accident claims that resulted in lost work time
  - Safety practices currently in place at the firm
  - Knowledge base at the state university

Intellectual Content

Re-creating the intellectual content would require the services of at least one experienced individual. The person selected was an Aria manager with 15 years' experience in safety and avoiding job-related accidents. To his salary ($100,000 per year) were added overhead, support, and benefits of approximately $50,000. The safety concepts presented in the DVD were expected to provide relevant training to Aria employees for the next five years. Thereafter, technological innovation would likely render existing safety concepts and practices obsolete. Projecting a five-year intellectual development period with total annual costs of approximately $150,000 resulted in an estimated total cost of $750,000 for the safety instruction. Based on discussions with management and taking into account the estimated five-year benefit period, it was determined that 25% of the total expenditures related to the covered safety instruction concepts and information included in the DVD; this provided a replacement cost of approximately $187,500 for the intellectual content.

Cost Summary

Aria's demonstration workforce consisted of two managers and eight employees for six weeks, as shown in Table 7.3.

TABLE 7.3 Fair Value of Aria's Training DVD ($)

Salaries	45,000
Overhead and benefits	21,000
Equipment, gasoline, and administration	15,000
	81,000
Producer's fee	75,000
Subtotal	156,000
Intellectual content	
Experienced individual	100,000
Overhead support and benefits	50,000
Total	150,000
Less nonsafety portion	0
Net	150,000
Development period	5 years
Total intellectual content costs	750,000
Portion related to DVD	25%
Intellectual content of DVD	187,500
Total costs of DVD	343,500
Portion applicable to transferred rights	40%
Value of DVD for transfer	137,400
Rounded to closest $5,000	135,000

Software Systems

Subsequently, Aria's parent, Greensleeves, was acquired by Andus Inc., a conglomerate. One of Greensleeves's significant intangible assets was the source code for various internally developed computer systems that ran its numerous service businesses. This software was made up of 225 programs comprising about 217,000 lines of code in nine systems, shown in Table 7.4.

In making its purchase price allocation after the acquisition, Andus adopted the cost approach for the fair value of the software because:

▪ While there are a number of enterprise resource planning (ERP) systems that supply similar functionality, the Greensleeves systems are simpler, easier to maintain, and suitable to be rolled out to Andus's other units.
▪ All direct, indirect, and opportunity costs that relate to the creation of the software are reasonably determinable.
▪ The software was not created for sale, and management was not able to quantify the efficiencies it generated.
▪ The code was written in C++ to run on Linux, and used a number of public domain routines and programs.

Based on a sample review of every tenth file, the number of person-days required to re-create and test the code was estimated, as was the portion considered obsolete. The fully loaded cost per person-day was based on the expected

TABLE 7.4 Time to Re-Create Software

	Programs	Lines of Code	Daily Production	Person-Days to Re-Create
Capital assets	6	300	4.0	75
General ledger	28	4,225	13.0	325
Human resources	29	3,186	11.0	290
Order entry	10	1,541	7.0	220
Payables	6	403	4.0	100
Payroll	62	2,660	3.8	700
Production	61	24,518	10.5	2,335
Quality control	9	40,000	40.0	1,000
Receivables	14	900	6.0	150
	225	77,733	15.0	5,195

TABLE 7.5 Fair Values of Greensleeves Systems

Obsolete %	System	Person- Days	Fully Loaded Cost ($)	Reproduction Cost ($000)	Value ($000)
35	Production	2,335	380	887	577
25	Human resources	290	100	116	87
15	General ledger	325	400	130	111
15	Payables	100	400	40	34
15	Receivables	150	400	60	51
10	Payroll	700	425	298	268
10	Order entry	220	450	99	89
5	Capital assets	75	400	30	29
5	Quality control	1,000	475	475	451
		5,195	411	2,135	1,696
	Rounded				1,700

number of each of three classes of programmers required—junior, experienced, and superior (see Tables 7.4 and 7.5).

By the replacement cost method, the value of the software is $1,700,000 rounded. To confirm this is a reasonable estimate of fair value, two questions must be asked: "What deductions, if any, need to be made for the four factors?" and "Would market participants be willing to pay this amount?" The four factors are functional deterioration, technological obsolescence, physical decline, and economic deprivation. Of those, the only one that might have an effect is technological obsolescence due to the mature nature of the programming language (C++) and operating system (Linux).

After reviewing the well-maintained and well-commented code with an expert adviser, management determined that a 10% reduction to $1,530,000 should be made for this factor. With respect to an exit price, similar commercially available, complex installations would have license fees of between $1,200,000 and $1,500,000 for the number of users contemplated by Andus, including those currently operated by Greensleeves; therefore, based on using a competitive product, a reduced amount of $1,500,000 qualifies as fair value.

Assembled Workforce

Although an assembled workforce often meets the criteria to be an intangible asset and was treated as such in the United States until 2001, FASB determined

TABLE 7.6 Aria Assembled Workforce Replacement Cost Method

Job Grade	Payroll ($000)	Cost to Recruit	Cost to Train	Replacement Cost ($000)
A1	185.5	5%	10%	27.8
A2	255.8	10%	15%	64.0
A3	455.1	15%	20%	159.3
A4	291.6	20%	25%	131.2
	1,188.0			382.3
B1	298.5	10%	20%	89.6
B2	157.2	15%	25%	62.9
B3	453.7	20%	30%	226.9
B4	810.6	25%	40%	526.9
	1,720.0			906.2
C1	836.6	20%	35%	460.1
C2	591.6	25%	50%	443.7
C3	845.4	30%	50%	676.3
C4	427.0	35%	50%	363.0
	2,700.6			1,943.1
D1	557	35%	45%	445.6
D2	367.8	40%	50%	331.0
D3	493.9	40%	55%	469.2
D4	961.3	40%	60%	961.3
	2,380.0			2,207.1
Total	7,988.6			5,438.7

that it no longer qualified because the normal methods of measurement do not result in an exit price and hence the result is not fair value. However, it is treated as a contributory asset in valuing many intangibles, especially brands, and therefore a supportable amount needs to be developed. Several methods and techniques from the cost and income approaches are used to value assembled workforces (see Table 7.6). The most common are the replacement costs relating to the individuals involved, including:

- Salaries and benefits of employees involved in recruiting and interviewing
- Overhead and benefit costs related to them
- Headhunter fees
- Direct hiring expenditures such as job placement ads and relocation costs
- Learning curve adjustment as employee's effectiveness improves over time
- On-the-job and off-site training expenses

The estimated costs to recruit, hire, and train new employees are expressed as a percentage of their total annual compensation; the learning curve is the period new hires take to become fully effective from an initial assumed 50% efficiency. When there is a job grade system, total compensation for a grade is calculated by multiplying the number of individuals by their average salary and related benefits. Table 7.6 shows Aria's management's estimated costs to recruit and train employees for each grade: It shows a value of $5,440,000 (rounded) for the assembled workforce or 68% of the annual payroll.

 CONCLUSION

Although the FASB and IASB prefer actual prices in active markets (Chapter 6) or "a present value technique" such as discounted cash flows (Chapter 8) because they more easily reflect the assumptions of market participants, methods under the cost approach provide essential information to establish the reasonableness of value indications from other approaches.

CHAPTER EIGHT

The Income Approach to Fair Value

There are very few things which we know which are not capable of being reduced to a mathematical reasoning, and when they cannot, it's a sign that our knowledge of them is very small and confused.

—*John Arbuthnot (1667–1735), British mathematician*

N THIS CHAPTER, we come to the third and, in many ways, most important set of valuation methods, the income approach to fair value. Sometimes described as "the very basics of value," these methods are the most common. Almost every day there is a reference to a price to earnings ratio (PER) in most newspapers' business sections, and the basic discounted cash flow (DCF) value is constantly used by investment bankers.

There are two sets of methods under the income approach. The first, which goes back to the seventeenth century, is the capitalization of the current or projected benefits. Originally it was dividends or other distributions; now it is either the current or next year's forecast net income or cash flow (usually expressed as earnings per share—EPS) by a PER, which reflects the level of interest rates, the risks involved, and the anticipated growth. As most readers are familiar with capitalization methods, we will not spend much time on them.

The more complex DCF method is described by the Financial Accounting Standards Board (FASB) and the International Accounting Standards Board (IASB) as a present value technique. In this, the current value of an asset is the total of all the present values of the net cash receipts or disbursements anticipated from the item during its remaining useful life (RUL—see Chapter 7); for a corporation this is usually considered infinite. The present value of each periodic (normally annual) contribution is calculated by discounting it to the valuation date at a rate that takes into account the level of interest rates, the risks involved, and a factor reflecting the difficulties of long-term financial projections; the anticipated growth has been reflected in the projected cash flows. Normally it is undertaken by projecting annual net cash flows for several years (usually five), and then adding a terminal amount that represents the balance of the RUL; all of those figures are then discounted to the present.

 ## CAPITALIZATION METHODS

This well-known method of valuing anything is to capitalize its contemplated benefits. It is best done by developing a market-based capitalization rate, the reciprocal of the PER. The arithmetic is simple: A PER of 12.2 times results in a capitalization rate of 8.2% (100/12.2). Another way of expressing capitalization rates is the Gordon growth model, a modern version of a traditional technique, resurrected by Myron J. Gordon in 1962. It states that the capitalization rate is the risk-reflecting discount rate, less the expected growth.

This concept makes it easy to estimate an appropriate discount rate for virtually any quoted entity. Consider the shares of a well-known enterprise, Ford Motor Company, which, unlike General Motors or Chrysler, did not go bankrupt in the recession of 2008–2010. On April 26, 2011, Ford's common shares closed at $15.66 on the New York Stock Exchange (NYSE), giving the family-controlled firm a market capitalization of $58.3 billion. In 2010, the reported EPS figure was $1.91 for a PER of 8.2 times and a capitalization rate of 12.2%. Bank of America Merrill Lynch (BAML), a market participant's view, estimated Ford's future EPS at $2.30 for 2011, $2.12 for 2012, and $2.33 for 2013. With an expected five-year EPS growth from 2010 of 5.3%, the implied discount rate is 17.5% (the capitalization rate of 12.2% plus the EPS growth of 5.3%).

Later in this chapter, we discuss the weighted average cost of capital (WACC). For Ford, BAML calculates this at 13.6%, based on the market-driven, implicit discount rate. In 2010, based on BAML figures, Ford's return on capital employed (business enterprise value—BEV) was only 14.5%; this is projected to rise to 20% in 2011 and then decline to 13.4% in 2012 and 12.6% in 2013; in the latter years, no shareholder value is being created.

My preferred approach in selecting an applicable discount rate is to find comparable public companies from the large numbers of entities in many industries traded on the world's stock markets (see Chapter 6). The selected implicit capitalization rates are then adjusted for the differences in size, growth, risk, and marketability from the subject. In addition to finding comparables (not always as easy as it sounds), it is desirable to include a buildup method.

Buildup Method

A common method of obtaining a capitalization rate is to build it up from these six components:

1. *Risk-free rate.* Commonly the yield on 10-year government bonds of the particular country is used to reflect the opportunity cost of an investment in a closely held entity.
2. *Equity risk premium.* The expected extra rate of return of a diversified equity portfolio (in the United States the Standard & Poor's 500) over the risk-free rate is a forward-looking concept known as the equity risk premium (ERP). As it is unobservable in the market, estimates are typically derived from the long-term historical premiums applicable to equity securities over a risk-free rate. Measures of the premium for a number of countries may be obtained from work done by Credit Suisse, Morningstar, or Duff & Phelps.
3. *Industry risk adjustment.* One measure of such risks, used by the capital asset pricing model (CAPM), is a stock's beta, the relative price volatility of a share in relation to the index for the stock market on which it is traded.
4. *Size premium.* The size premium reflects the fact that investors consider small firms riskier but potentially more rewarding than large ones. According to Morningstar, the size premium in the United States ranges from a negative 0.36% for the largest 10% of those listed on the NYSE to about 9.50% for the smallest 5%; the swing is close to 10 percentage points.

5. *Specific risks.* If a beta, which is not available for private companies, is not applied, the capitalization rate has to be adjusted to reflect size and industry risks, as well as those risks specific to the entity. A useful technique is to look at certain areas of the business and add a premium of between 0.0% and 4.0% for the perceived risks in each of the following: location, product range, capitalization (debt/equity ratio), technology in use, industry ease of entry, profit margins and their variability, customer or supplier dependence, environmental impact, management capabilities, and regulatory situation.

6. *Growth prospects.* As shown in Table 8.1, the earnings/growth prospects of the entity are then deducted to give the capitalization rate. This should be the annual percentage growth in net income reasonably achievable for the next five years; for private firms, it rarely exceeds 5% including inflation, although higher figures were achieved in the middle of the recent decade.

TABLE 8.1   Example of Buildup Capitalization Rate

	Capitalization Rate (%)
10-year government bond yield	4.5
Equity risk premium	6.5
Size premium	2.5
Specific risks	
Location	0.5
Product range	1.0
Capitalization	1.0
Technology in use	0.5
Industry ease of entry	0.0
Profit margins	1.0
Dependence	1.0
Environmental impact	0.5
Management	1.5
Regulatory situation	0.0
Subtotal	20.5
Growth rate	(2.0)
Capitalization rate	18.5
PER	5.4

International Equity Risk Premiums

Table 8.2 shows international equity risk premiums for 19 countries over various periods of up to 111 years, based on data in the Credit Suisse Global Investor Return Yearbook 2011. Unlike Ibbotson or Duff & Phelps, the data is after inflation. Therefore when using it to develop a capitalization rate, an estimate of the current inflation rate for the particular country has to be added. The negative figures in recent years reflect the outstanding performance of most government bond markets. To a great extent this was the result of the general acceleration of government antirecession spending since 2007 and the activities of many central banks to lower interest rates.

TABLE 8.2   Real Equity Premiums versus Bonds

Country	2001–2010 10 years	1986–2010 25 years	1961–2010 50 years	1900–2010 111 years
Australia	2.7%	0.5%	3.5%	5.9%
Belgium	−4.7%	0.2%	1.0%	2.6%
Canada	−0.9%	−0.7%	1.7%	3.7%
Denmark	0.9%	0.7%	1.2%	2.0%
Finland	−7.3%	4.6%	4.6%	5.6%
France	−6.0%	0.0%	−0.9%	3.2%
Germany	−4.3%	−0.8%	−0.1%	5.4%
Ireland	−6.2%	0.5%	3.5%	2.9%
Italy	−7.3%	−3.7%	−1.9%	3.7%
Japan	−5.2%	−5.3%	−1.4%	5.0%
Netherlands	−7.1%	1.7%	3.3%	3.5%
New Zealand	1.1%	−4.5%	2.2%	3.8%
Norway	3.1%	1.0%	2.8%	2.5%
South Africa	5.8%	1.5%	6.9%	5.5%
Spain	1.3%	4.6%	3.4%	2.3%
Sweden	0.3%	3.1%	4.8%	3.8%
Switzerland	−4.2%	2.4%	2.1%	2.1%
United Kingdom	−1.3%	1.0%	3.4%	3.9%
United States	−3.9%	0.9%	2.6%	4.4%
Global	−4.0%	−0.8%	1.2%	3.8%

In addition to a probable reversal of recent exceptionally low interest rates, one must take into consideration the apparent Kondratiev (50- to 60-year) cycle in bond yields. In 49 years (1962–2010) yields on 10-year U.S. Treasury notes rose from 3.99% on January 4, 1962, to a peak of 13.99% on May 29, 1984—an increase of 1,000 basis points (a basis point, or bp, equals one-hundredth of a percentage point) in 22 years, representing 45.5 bp annually. It was followed by a decline to a low of 2.41% on October 6, 2010, a drop of 1,158 bp in 26 years or 44.5 bp annually. The similar upward and downward movements do not imply a return to double-digit rates but, as suggested by Milan Kundera (1929–) a Czech author, "Happiness is the longing for repetition."

In 2010, some analysts adjusted the risk-free rate to reflect the impact of the Federal Reserve's quantitative easing programs. Another technique that avoids the need to increase the historical ERP is to reflect the higher risks attached to shares by creating a synthetic risk-free 10-year rate of 4.05% starting with the two-year Treasury note (recently 0.45%) and adding 45 bp a year for the additional eight-year term.

INCOME APPROACH—DISCOUNTING

The preferred method under the income approach is to discount future cash flows, as the resulting DCF value is totally forward-looking. As in all valuation methods, an essential element for determining DCF values is internal consistency. The selected discount rate must be appropriate for the projected cash flows. Those may be either operating cash flows before financing costs or net cash flows after all costs and expenditures, whether operating, investing, or financing; each must include only items directly related to the business and requires a different discount rate. As management is responsible for determining fair values, it must be able to logically support choosing either operating cash flows or net cash flows.

Discount Rates

Risks are traditionally dealt with by adopting a risk-adjusted discount rate (RADR). As shown by the Ford example, this is implicitly given to quoted shares by stock markets. The larger the perceived risks attached to the future cash flows, the higher the RADR and the lower the present values; the process is the same as that used to value a bond after it has been categorized by an established rating agency.

In 2000, FASB concluded that focusing on determining discount rates "commensurate with the risks involved" was unproductive and that it is preferable to include at least part, if not all, the risks in the projected cash flows. To achieve this goal, two alternative methods may be applied. The first is expected cash flows, recommended in FASB's Concepts Statement No. 7, *Using Cash Flow Information and Present Value in Accounting Measurements;* the second is the more recently developed probability cash flows, similar to the use of scenarios (discussed in Chapter 4); as neither is in general use, they are not dealt with in this chapter. Equity-level cash flows, in particular, should be discounted at the entity's cost of equity capital discussed earlier. Operating cash flows that result in a total enterprise value are commonly discounted using WACC.

Weighted Average Cost of Capital

The concept of using WACC is based on the premise that the value of a business cannot be changed by how it is financed. This was developed by Eugene Fama and Kenneth French, both winners of the Nobel Prize for economics. Applying it requires separating the firm's operating activities from its financing by adjusting net cash flows to remove all interest and other financial costs. The tax benefits from the deductibility of interest are taken into consideration separately, as are all borrowings and debt repayments. WACC reflects the advantage of the lower after-tax cost of debt. It is calculated by taking into account the costs of debt and equity for comparable enterprises and management's planned capital structure, which may vary over time.

Calculating WACC

Calculating WACC requires three amounts:

1. The cost of equity
2. Its proportion of the invested capital
3. The after-tax cost of debt

The mathematical formula is:

$$\text{WACC} = [1 - D/(D + E)] \times K_e + [D/(D + E) \times K_d \times (1 - T)]$$

where:
K_e = Required equity return
K_d = Cost of debt for the type of firm with planned capital structure

D = Fair value of debt
E = Fair value of equity
T = Effective tax rate

To establish the percentages of the fair values of the debt and equity, approximations are often used. For firms with good credit ratings, the face amount of their floating-rate and fixed-rate medium-term (up to five years) obligations is acceptable. Fixed-rate long-term liabilities are aggregated and valued, taking into account the entity's credit standing (see Chapter 11). The fair value of the equity is normally obtained by the market approach or a capitalization rate developed by a buildup method. If the entity is issuing or, more commonly, retiring debt, the proportion of debt and equity in the capital structure may need to be recalculated each year. General practice has been to assume that retired debt is replaced by new borrowings; that may be true for an enterprise as a whole, but is unlikely for a particular reporting or cash-generating unit.

A simplified example of calculating WACC is shown in Table 8.3.

This technique is suitable for general manufacturing and service businesses. For start-ups, turnarounds, or high-tech firms, private market or venture capital rates of return are used as the cost of equity.

Effect of Leverage on WACC

As the amount of low-cost debt is increased and that of high-cost equity decreased, WACC declines. However, fair value cannot be increased simply by adding debt, because as the proportion of debt rises, so do the risks and hence the required equity rate of return. At some point, any reductions in WACC from

TABLE 8.3 Simplified Calculation of WACC

Category	Fair Value ($000)	Share (%)	Cost (%)	Contribution (%)
Bank	500			
Bonds	2,030			
Total debt	2,530	44.4	3.3[a]	1.46
Equity	3,170	55.6	16.3[b]	9.06
Total invested capital	5,700	100		11.52

[a] After tax at 36%.
[b] Obtained by a buildup technique applied to an estimated value from another valuation method.

adding additional debt will be more than offset by the higher cost of equity that takes into account the shareholders' perceived risks. Most valuation practitioners believe that WACC is constant within plus or minus 5% at the optimum debt/equity ratio for any particular industry. However, if the capital structure is substantially altered, for example when debt is repaid or borrowing greatly increased, the risks involved and the required return on the equity will also change.

Changes in WACC

In valuing reporting or cash-generating units for impairment testing, management has the flexibility to adjust WACC over time, taking into consideration factors that may affect the cost of debt or equity:

- ▪ Unusual and temporary situations, as in leveraged projects when the debt proportion of the capital structure is expected to fall significantly and relatively fast; the costs of either or both components may start at high levels and decline sharply.
- ▪ Periods when interest rates are expected to change. An example is when short-term interest rates exceed long-term ones. After a period, the conventional situation (where rates gradually go up as the term increases) will likely return.
- ▪ Periods when equity returns are below those of long-term debt, such as in the late 1990s.

The use of WACC as the discount rate is most suitable in situations where a firm, a reporting or cash-generating unit, or a particular asset such as real estate is funded by a mixture of debt and equity. As intangible assets are not normally financed with debt, they are usually valued using an adjusted equity rate. However, if the entity has been able to obtain such borrowings, a modified WACC, using only the relevant loans, may be applied.

Selecting the Capital Structure

In determining WACC, a valuator will make assumptions regarding the capital structure of the entity. There are basically three alternatives: the current situation, management's planned position, and decreasing debt as existing borrowings are repaid when due and not refinanced. The capital structure of a reporting or cash-generating unit selected to calculate its WACC will have an impact on the fair value in two ways: first, on the discount rate, and second, on the extent of nonoperating assets.

For a reporting or cash-generating unit with significant cash or marketable securities, management should examine future working capital requirements and may conclude that a portion is a nonoperating asset that, if the entity is a free-standing business, could be distributed to shareholders. The amount that might reasonably be withdrawn depends on many factors, including the unit's capacity to bear additional debt and the willingness of banks to fund it. The choice of the capital structure is essential to calculate WACC but not an equity discount rate.

Private Market Rates

All relevant facts, expectations, and assumptions concerning the risks of the cash flows and the nature of the business are traditionally reflected in the discount rate. Table 8.4 shows the ranges of private market and venture capital equity returns (discount rates) commonly seen in the United States during 2010 according to a study by John Paglia of Pepperdine University.

At various times in the past decade, both short- and long-term interest rates decreased significantly and stayed low for a considerable period. However, the rates of return required by investors in smaller private companies did not

TABLE 8.4 Private Equity and Venture Capital Rates of Return

	Gross Annualized Rates		
	Quartile I	Median	Quartile III
Private Equity			
$1 million EBITDA	25.0%	**30.0%**	30.8%
$5 million EBITDA	25.0%	**30.0%**	30.0%
$10 million EBITDA	24.5%	**30.0%**	31.3%
$25 million EBITDA	25.0%	**28.0%**	30.0%
$50 million EBITDA	22.0%	**25.0%**	30.0%
Venture Capital			
Seed	30.0%	**50.0%**	100.0%
Start-up	30.0%	**40.0%**	75.0%
Early stage	25.0%	**35.0%**	50.0%
Expansion	20.0%	**30.0%**	40.0%
Later stage	20.0%	**30.0%**	35.0%

(continued)

TABLE 8.4 *(Continued)*

	Gross Annualized Rates		
	Quartile I	Median	Quartile III
Effective WACC for U.S. Manufacturers			
$1 million EBITDA		18.6%	
$5 million EBITDA		17.6%	
$10 million EBITDA		16.6%	
$25 million EBITDA		16.4%	
$50 million EBITDA		9.9%	
$100 million EBITDA		8.1%	

show a parallel trend; to a large extent they reflected increases in the pricing of the risks taken into account in a buildup capitalization rate such as:

- Dependence on few products
- Swings in revenue growth
- State of product development
- Depth of management
- Technological strengths and weaknesses
- Competition

TERMINAL AMOUNTS

As discussed in Chapter 5, "Projecting What Is to Come," it is very difficult to prepare supportable financial forecasts or projections for more than five years. Therefore, a DCF model typically consists of two stages; the first is individual projections for each of the first few years, the second is a terminal amount that represents the present value of all future cash flows expected during its RUL.

The most common means of calculating a terminal amount is by using the Gordon growth model discussed earlier in this chapter. This capitalizes the net income (not cash flows) for the last projected year at an appropriate capitalization rate giving the expected value of the entity at the end of the projection period.

Two other methods are in common use; the first is applicable when growth at the end of the projection period is still high, say 8% to 10% annually, but is expected to revert to normal (around 3% a year) reasonably soon. The purpose of this method is to add an additional stage, extending the projected period by naive forecasts based on growth declining by between 0.5 and 1.0 percentage points per year, until reaching a steady state. The Gordon growth model is then applied to the resulting net income to give a terminal amount.

The second method, mainly applicable to technology firms, is to assume no effective value at the end of the RUL of the major asset (e.g., a patent) and, after projecting to that date (assuming a notional liquidation), the tangible net worth is used as the terminal amount.

Management should consider the technique selected to establish the terminal amount when choosing the applicable equity discount rate. Such levels can vary considerably, depending on investor enthusiasm for a particular industry and general economic conditions. Smaller entities, with revenues under $100 million, whether independent businesses, reporting units, or cash-generating units, tend to require higher discount rates.

Chapter 4 demonstrated with a simplified DCF model the effect of choosing market participants' assumptions over those of management in calculating fair values. The characteristics of the DCF model depend on the nature of the entity; however, it is important that all nonrealized profits, such as from mark-to-market activities, included in net income are removed from the cash flows. All write-downs need careful review to determine the effect, if any, they have on future cash flows.

In most cases, discounting of annual cash flows is done on a midyear convention, as funds are expected to be generated equally during the year. Retailers and other organizations with cash flows skewed to the last quarter are normally discounted on a year-end basis.

Discounting operating cash flows, ignoring the effect of how the business is financed, is an important alternative to capitalizing OPEBITDA or OPEBITRAD as a means of obtaining a firm's BEV (see Chapter 6).

APPLICATION TO INTANGIBLE ASSETS

The available cash flows from an intangible asset depend completely on its RUL. If it is greater than the projection period, a terminal amount may be appropriate; but preferably, and especially if the extra time is short, a naive extension is added to the projection period. In discounting such cash flows, an appropriate rate of return is selected. This will not usually be the entity's WACC, but one that, in addition to the general level of interest rates, reflects adjustments for the perceived financial and business risks of the relevant assets. It is likely to be between 120% and 150% of the entity's cost of equity, arrived at by a buildup method.

Financial and Business Risks

Every discount rate should consider the financial and business risks specific to the intangible asset and the activities to which it relates. Examples include:

- The industry outlook
- The characteristics of the asset
- Alternate uses for the asset
- Licensing opportunities
- The entity's financial risks
- Diversification of existing operations
- Depth of management
- Access to capital markets
- Geographic diversification
- Risks related to contributing assets
- Number of years in business

Selecting Intangible Discount Rates

Discount rates for assets, particularly intangibles, vary greatly. For an established, widely licensed patent portfolio, the industry average may be suitable, while an emerging technological area with high obsolescence will likely require a return similar to that demanded by venture capitalists. Establishing such rates is a two-step process. First, management develops a discount rate applicable to the equity of the entity as a whole. Then it establishes specific rates for its various assets by identifying and quantifying their risks relative to those of the entity and of similar items available in the market.

Conceptually, the discount rate for the business may be viewed as a weighted average of those appropriate to the individual assets. Those discount rates will range from very low for cash to high for goodwill, the most risky. A discount rate may also be derived from an existing capitalization rate by adding back the projected average annual compound growth of the benefits stream.

Weighted Average Return on Assets

While WACC is calculated after tax, the weighted average return on assets (WARA) is a pretax measure. However, it is very useful as a means of supporting a chosen enterprise discount rate. For a WARA analysis, each major asset class is assigned a market (risk-adjusted) rate of return; those are then reconciled to the rate of return for the entity as a whole. In general, the residual return on goodwill is higher than that for any other asset.

Example: Grange Lighting WARA

Based on its acquisition due diligence, management of the buyer determines that the newly acquired Grange Lighting Company has significant unrecorded assets as well as goodwill. Those include fully depreciated molds and dies with continuing value, as well as the intangible assets of its brand name, customer relationships, order backlog, and core technology. Any of them could be transferred independently to a willing buyer without having to sell the entire company.

On acquisition, Grange had no borrowings and a modest cash position; it was acquired for $8 million cash at a capitalization rate of 10% based on sustainable net income of $800,000. Before income tax at 36%, the pretax profit was $1.25 million for a related pretax return on investment (ROI) of 15.6%; this is the WARA of the entity as a whole.

The intangible assets, brand name, customer relationships, core technologies, and order backlog are all potentially transferable. However, analyzing them suggests that, due to competition from imports, they are exposed to significantly greater risks than is the overall business. The buyer's purchase price allocation process results in the fair values and returns shown in Table 8.5.

TABLE 8.5 Reconciliation of WARA

Assets	Fair Value ($000)	Rate of Return (%)	Pretax Return ($000)
Current			
Cash and equivalents	110	1.5	1.7
Receivables	1,150	7.0	80.5
Inventories	1,080	8.0	86.4
Prepaids and other	100	9.0	9.0
Total current assets	2,440	7.3	177.6
Capital			
Property, plant, & equipment	1,850	11.0	203.5
Molds and dies	750	13.0	97.5
Intangible			
Brand name	800	17.2	137.6

(continued)

TABLE 8.5 *(Continued)*

Assets	Fair Value ($000)	Rate of Return (%)	Pretax Return ($000)
Customer relationships	1,250	17.2	215.0
Core technology	1,000	17.2	172.0
Order backlog	230	15.6	35.9
Goodwill	1,030	20.5	211.0
Total assets	9,350	134	1,250.0
Current liabilities	(1,350)	—	—
Purchase price	8,000	15.6	1,250.0

The intangible assets were each allocated 17.2% (110% of the WARA), while the rate for goodwill (20.5%) is obtained by dividing its return (obtained by deducting those for the other assets from that of the entity) by the residual return allocated to it. ▪

Incremental Profitability

The incremental profitability technique establishes the value of some intangible assets by comparing the operating performance of the business that owns them with comparable firms that do not, from which the incremental profit from owning the assets can be derived. It is then capitalized at a suitable rate to determine value. This is not commonly used as a primary method, since it requires intricate assumptions, detailed comparisons, and numerous subjective judgments.

Adjustments for Control

There has been a great deal of discussion and diversity of practice in the worldwide valuation community as to whether a DCF calculation represents the value of a controlling or a noncontrolling interest and if a control premium (or in certain circumstances a discount for lack of control) should be applied. A related issue is whether such a discount is appropriate when the subject interest has no possibility of obtaining control. The difference could significantly affect the related estimate of fair value, since observed control premiums often exceed 20%.

The willingness of a third party to pay a premium for control of a business depends on a number of factors. Perhaps the most important is the ability of the buyer to achieve operational improvements, either through synergies available to all market participants or through special factors, such as an adjacent plant, available solely to the particular buyer. In order to determine whether a DCF value justifies a control premium, it is necessary to understand the underlying performance of the company and, if possible, market participants' view about any additional amount they might pay.

Financial projections used for fair values include 100% of the expected operating cash flows of the entity and, although based on expected market participants' assumptions, should be consistent with management's policies and decision making regarding operations, reinvestment, and intended distributions. Acquisition valuations include the benefits available to market participants from potential synergies of a combination of the target with the acquirer.

A DCF value is based on applying a discount rate to the projected cash flows. It reflects the time value of money, as well as elements of systematic (or nondiversified) risk inherent in the uncertain cash flows; it also incorporates the concepts of leverage and optimal capital structure. Since only a controlling shareholder can affect company policies and decisions required to obtain the benefits of synergies, the benefits (and incremental value) of control are inherent in the projections. Therefore, in our view, DCF analyses reflect the fair value of a controlling interest.

CHAPTER NINE

Sources of Value—Profits

Innovation distinguishes between leader and follower.

—*Steve Jobs (1955–2011), American entrepreneur*

A PERENNIAL QUESTION asked by countless boards of directors is: "How can we improve the value of the firm?" There are only two possible answers—increase benefits/profits/cash flows, or lower capitalization or discount rates by greater expected growth or reduced risks. The former is more significant, as growth, resulting mainly from innovation and the elimination of money-losing operations and customers, improves both profits and capitalization rates. This chapter deals with the profit side of the equation; the next will cover risks.

 ## STRUCTURE OF BUSINESSES

Nearly every business has a set of existing operations; most have, as well, emerging activities and future opportunities; as previously discussed in Chapter 4, all are sources of value. Emerging activities are projects in the course of becoming businesses. A common example is an in-process research and development (IPR&D) project being tested before general release; others are planned extensions of product lines or expansions into new geographic markets. Future opportunities are more nebulous, but certainly include early-stage innovative prospects expected to be profitable but far from proven, as well as potential new products or services together with markets in the course of investigation. The latter may turn out to be "pie in the sky"—that is, not a business—but, if successful, may have a potential major impact on the entity.

In establishing the fair value of a reporting unit or cash-generating unit, all costs and any recoveries relating to emerging activities or future opportunities should be excluded from the figures for existing operations. Each of them, if significant, is valued separately, often including some real-option techniques to take into account their potential.

 ## INNOVATION

Innovation is a process that, with luck, creates intangible assets for the entity engaged in it, although because they are internally generated, innovations will never be recorded on its financial statements; the activity also reduces reported profits but often increases fair values. The three-phase process described in this section underlies all innovations, which, by their nature, also involve significant risks. The material is based on an article, "The Three Phases of Value Capture," by Rhonda Germany and Raman Mualidharan of Booz & Company, an international consulting firm, published in *Strategy + Business* magazine, first quarter 2001.

In most fields, innovation is an essential part of future opportunities and emerging activities. It is therefore of considerable importance for management to understand the process. To help all of us do just that, Generate Companies, a consultancy, created the World Database of Innovation (www.generatecompanies.com). Its two sections, "Best Practices in Innovation" and "Innovation Experts," are comprehensive collections of innovation methods, research, literature, and trends; its aim is to help the world better understand what works and what does not; it is often helpful in dealing with early-stage companies.

Phase 1: Proving Feasibility

Proving feasibility is the first phase of the innovation process. In this phase, a new product/process/service is developed, tested, and brought to market. Often, early adopters accept it; however, sometimes it falls on its face. Its usefulness tends to be scattered and unfocused, with profits not expected until sometime in the future. For example, in the 1990s when General Electric developed a plastic for lightweight but strong automobile bumpers, it discovered that most of the industry's existing molding machines were not capable of making them. It therefore had to work with equipment manufacturers to develop an infrastructure that would allow all participants—resin suppliers, molders, component makers, and auto assemblers—to collaboratively achieve the advantages of less weight, lower cost, and improved fuel consumption.

Early adopter customers may offer valuable feedback, which helps management hone capabilities, develop sources, and create distribution channels. In this phase, innovators are likely to share information freely and pay limited attention to who owns what intellectual property. For example, in the early days of the PC, an unknown individual stole and distributed the BASIC computer language that Bill Gates and Paul Allen had written for their fledgling company, Microsoft. Some hobbyists, fans of an early computer called the Altair, were annoyed that the firm was selling rather than giving away this vital enabling tool.

In the long run, innovations have a better chance of succeeding if someone has the vision and discipline to mold them into a profitable business. In Phase 1, a key factor is quick determination of where profits are likely to be achieved and how to encourage growth. An entity must choose which technologies, products, and markets to pursue, using techniques such as decision trees or real-option analyses, both of which are beyond the scope of this book.

Phase 2: Defining the Business

In the second phase, defining the business, an entity must determine where value is most likely to be realized within the supply chain. In the past, profits from controlling a patent or through customer access depended on information not available to others. In a manufacturing-oriented economy, this could create a competitive advantage for decades. Currently, those situations and related profits still arise but tend to last only for short periods, perhaps merely months. The need to protect intellectual property and achieve a satisfactory return is therefore vital.

Growing standardization, together with strong intellectual property laws and supportive public policy, are part of this phase. For example, in the U.S. radio industry, the technology was standardized and the number of broadcasting licenses restricted during the 1920s. The intellectual property framework created by station owners negotiating royalties with musicians' unions enabled the fledgling business to flourish alongside the strong existing record industry.

As markets select certain technologies, the number of participants shrinks and competition increases among the survivors; they must balance the need to expand the overall industry with the imperative of securing their own position. This can be tricky; should they aim for higher volume or better margins? To decide, a firm must have a good grasp of supply and demand issues, difficult in a constantly changing environment.

Due to the need for quick funds or perhaps from shortsightedness, many organizations enter into deals that give away too much. For instance, IBM bet that the largest share of profit in PCs would accrue to branded hardware vendors, as it did with mainframes. In ceding the operating system to Microsoft, IBM lost out and helped turn the supplier into one of the world's dominant companies.

In this phase, an entity must develop a perception for how the industry might evolve. Although conventional strategic planning is difficult, managers should remember that operating principles and procedures will determine who makes money and how, as well as how much.

Strategies for Profits

At this stage, it is essential for a successful firm to keep a keen eye on the industry's progress and aim for profits. Usually, this involves following one of five strategies.

1. *Improvement.* Whoever can deliver better product performance succeeds. Does it work faster? Can it do something different? The value of new technology is high, and barriers to switching are low. In some technology-based industries (e.g., disk drives) frequent changes in expertise allow new participants to leapfrog over leaders. In others, such as microprocessors, the dominant player (Intel) has been able to maintain its position with ongoing innovation, even cannibalizing sales of its own successful product by continuously offering items that quickly become market leaders, while at the same time passing on declining costs to consumers.

2. *Value.* Whoever can deliver a "can't do without" product succeeds. Speed to market is critical, even if the product is not fully developed. While new technologies are valuable, they may present substantial barriers to customers wishing to switch products. This action usually involves costs, giving early winners a strong continuing position, even if competitors offer attractive features or a lower price. Although WordPerfect had been available for many years, Microsoft Office, with its integrated functionalities, added enough value to become the industry standard.

3. *Alignment.* Whoever can deliver the best price/service combination succeeds. This requires a well-defined market with limited barriers to entry and close to perfection in the product and/or service; winners develop business systems to fulfill the market's needs, achieve the highest possible quality in tests, and then roll them out. For example, Southwest Airlines created an Internet reservation system allowing it to dominate the short-haul budget-conscious market.

4. *Infrastructure.* Whoever owns the tangible asset or distribution network succeeds. An airline's landing slots, a cable television firm's wires, or an oil company's retail outlets can make switching almost prohibitive. As a result, innovation is less of a threat than regulation is, although relying on such protection can lead to complacency.

5. *Cost.* Whoever offers customers the best price succeeds. Where there are few barriers to changing suppliers, new technologies that lower costs can create a valuable edge. Many commodity chemical companies have been doing this for years.

Phase 3: Maximizing Returns

The third phase aims to maximize returns; possibly lasting for an extended period, it is about continuous enhancements centered on customer needs. In the past, it consisted largely of effectively executing a plan, keeping costs low and efficiencies high, exploiting pricing opportunities, and extending product offerings to new markets. Now, an entity must aggressively innovate and seize the slightest benefit created by any temporary advantage. The focus is on the highest returns on investment. There is no time to rest, as "there is nothing certain in life but change," according to American comedian Mel Brooks (1926–).

Fulfilling customers' expectations requires a firm to develop close links with suppliers, retailers, and customers; the objective is to make everybody part of the supply chain. This requires innovation in business systems, using the awareness of customer needs to develop product portfolios with varying reward/risk ratios. C. K. Prahalad and Venkatram Ramaswamy of the Harvard Business School state, "The market has become a forum in which consumers play an active role in creating and competing for value."

Value Constellations

Innovation is important in all industries, especially in those that are technology oriented, where the rapid dissemination of information forces constant adaptation. Alterations in supply chains can force firms to rethink how they get to market, what they need to own, and how to deal with suppliers and customers. Errors in those areas can have a significant effect on an entity's value.

The speed of change has considerable impact on this three-phase sequence. Innovations, such as microprocessors, the Internet, hyperstorage, and genomics, are transforming almost every industry primarily built on information, which today is abundant, ubiquitous, fast, and cheap. In "The Nature of the Firm," published in 1937 (*Economica* 4, no. 16), Ronald Coase, the 1991 Nobel laureate in economics, concluded that the boundaries of a business are defined by its transaction costs: "A firm will tend to expand until the costs of organizing an extra transaction within the firm become equal to the costs of carrying out the same transaction on the open market."

Then and frequently today, those costs are largely determined by the availability of information: Who can supply the needed goods? Can they produce the quantity required? What is the price? Are better terms available? Is superior quality accessible? Can faster delivery be guaranteed?

Hard-to-acquire or imperfect information contributes to high transaction costs, in turn leading firms to integrate vertically. At one time, it was cheaper for General Motors to build its parts in-house than to search the globe for cheaper suppliers. Today, as the costs of sharing and using information fall, according to Dr. Coase's theory, entities have strong incentives to concentrate on core capabilities and outsource other activities to the most appropriate supplier.

The result is that supply chains are now adding alliances to become value constellations. The best value-capture mechanisms often lie outside the individual firm, yet the value created by a dominant enterprise (such as Intel) is still essential to the viability of its entire industry.

Procter & Gamble's Approach

A January 2011 panel discussion in Singapore on "Asia Fuelling Global Innovation" featured Bruce Brown, Procter & Gamble's (P&G) chief technology officer and leader of its innovation program; Low Teck Seng, managing director of A*STAR; Maurizio Marchesini, P&G's vice president for research and development for Asia; Shamik Dasgupta, the regional head of Medtronic's Cardiac Rhythm Management business; Professor C. C. Hang of the National University of Singapore; and Deb Henretta, president of P&G Asia. The wide-ranging discussion about the general challenges facing companies in Asia and globally can be summarized by eight phrases:

1. *"For and amongst consumers."* Dr. Brown used this to describe how P&G will achieve its stated goal of serving five billion consumers by 2015 (an increase of 800 million); localizing research activities is a key component.
2. *"The red dot."* Mr. Low used this term to indicate how Singapore appears on a map. He stated that the country's small size allows it to be more nimble, reminding the audience that sometimes constraints can foster innovation.
3. *"Florence."* Dr. Marchesini noted similarities between Singapore and Florence during the Renaissance, with free-flowing ideas and disciplines colliding in both. He noted how solving tough problems requires interdisciplinary collocation where people work together in new ways.
4. *"Simplifying technology and new business models."* These are two ingredients Dr. Dasgupta described as vital for disruptive growth in markets like India and China.
5. *"Nonconsumption."* Professor Hang used the term to answer the question of where there are the greatest opportunities for disruptive growth in Asia. He noted that more than 20 million electric bikes were sold in China in 2010, many to women or other nontraditional vehicle purchasers.
6. *"As common as possible, as different as needed."* That's how Ms. Henretta described her approach to Asian markets. She pointed out real differences between consumers in different markets. For example, beauty means fair skin to many Asians and tanned skin to most U.S. consumers. Using scale where appropriate can help companies like P&G realize their full global potential.
7. *"Nonobvious disruptions."* Dr. Marchesini described how P&G sells a product under the Downy brand that provides long-lasting scent benefits to clothes, using microcapsules. In markets like the Philippines, this brings scent benefits to consumers who can't afford higher-end perfumes.
8. *"Reframe."* Ms. Henretta noted how important the process of reframing is in dealing with many of the challenges inherent in mastering innovation in today's economy. She noted one intriguing thing: "You have to make sure your workforce reflects the consumers you are going to serve."

Value Maps

Every manager lives in a world of perpetual motion, operating a business and planning to improve it at the same time. Every day means tough decisions, setting direction, allocating funds, and launching new initiatives to increase performance and create value. Value maps express the effects of innovation and help everyone involved focus on the right things, through a graphic view of what is to be done and why.

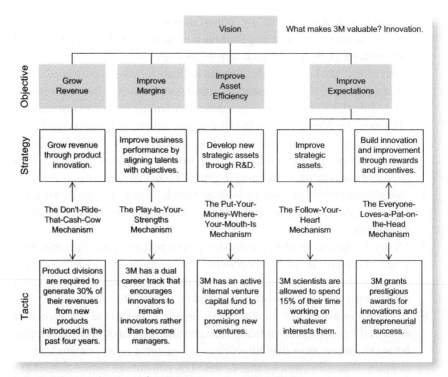

FIGURE 9.1　Value Map for 3M Company in the 1990s

Source: James C. Collins, "Aligning Action and Values," *Leader to Leader* 1 (Summer 1996): 19–24.

Figure 9.1 shows a value map for 3M Company, a major innovation-driven U.S. manufacturer. The top row, below "Vision," sets out four objectives that define actions to grow revenue and improve operating margins, asset efficiency, and expectations. The boxes under "Grow Revenue" and "Improve Margins" represent processes. Better operational performance is a result of making the business processes of generating revenue and controlling costs more effective and efficient. The "Improve Asset Efficiency" column requires increasing the effective use and efficiency of working capital as well as property, plant & equipment, in addition to developing new strategic assets through R&D resulting from innovation. Under "Improve Expectations," the capabilities of management and staff are key factors in a firm's consistent adaptation to changing business environments.

The bottom row shows tactics, with two basic types of actions. The first is to change what you do, alter strategy, and refocus resources. Maximizing value requires focusing on activities that provide the best returns from the available resources—a higher investment in profitable lines, discontinuing lower-profit products and services, and increased focus on high-value customers.

The second type of action is to do what you do better. Two paths to improve execution are streamlining or improving the processes or raising the efficiency and effectiveness of the people and technologies involved. Many things can be done to improve performance. No firm should try to pursue them all; just focus on what matters most. At a tactical level, setting priorities among actions depends on current operational performance, asset productivity, organizational capacities, and the importance to the firm of being strong in each particular area.

DUPONT ANALYSES

Another way to demonstrate the effects of innovation is a DuPont analysis. In the early years of the twentieth century, managers at E.I. du Pont de Nemours and Company in the United States, then the largest diversified chemical company in the world, developed tools to track the firm's financial and operating performance. Those look at profit margins and asset turnovers as the building blocks of return on assets. In its basic form, net income is adjusted by adding back interest, net of taxes, to obtain an amount DuPont calls "net income to invested capital." The objective is to avoid the measurement of an activity's performance being affected by how it is financed. The application of such analyses is another way to obtain higher benefits by improving the entity's use of resources. The formulas are:

$$\text{Return on Net Operating Assets} = \text{Profit Margin} \times \text{Asset Turnover}$$

$$\text{Profit Margin} = \frac{\text{Earnings Before Interest and Taxes}}{\text{Revenues}}$$

$$\text{Asset Turnover} = \frac{\text{Revenues}}{\text{Net Operating Assets}}$$

The concept is that returns can be improved by either higher profit margins (greater efficiency) or increased sales, without adding any new equipment or additional assets (better effectiveness).

Profit Margin Drivers

In applying a DuPont analysis to a reporting or cash-generating unit, it is important to establish its profit margin drivers; examples are:

Sales
▪ Market trends
▪ Customer feedback
▪ Advertising and marketing programs
▪ Product line extensions
▪ Volume patterns
▪ Pricing power

Direct Costs
▪ Product design
▪ Production capacity
▪ Manufacturing efficiencies
▪ Raw material choices
▪ Labor situation (costs/rigidities)
▪ Overhead utilization
▪ Technologies in use
▪ Outsourcing

Operating Expenses
▪ Warehousing and distribution
▪ Shipping
▪ Selling organization
▪ Administrative
▪ Overhead

Income Tax
▪ Reduction strategies

Each factor should be assessed in terms of strengths, weaknesses, opportunities, and threats (SWOT), in the same way as the firm's strategic planning. It is also important to analyze the factors in connection with operational gearing—the relationship of fixed to total operating costs assets—as well as financial leverage.

Asset Turnover Determinants

Most managers and valuators concentrate primarily on the income statement and tend to ignore the importance of efficient resource utilization, reflected in the asset turnover ratio. The following list contains some factors to consider when attempting to increase revenues from existing plant and working capital or when trying to reduce the financial, physical, and human resources required for the current volume. The analyses will follow SWOT techniques, which are beyond the scope of this book.

Receivables
- Customer base
- Industry practices
- Collection policies
- Discounts and allowances
- Billing process
- Loss exposure

Property, Plant & Equipment
- Current capacity
- De-bottlenecking programs
- Production and scheduling efficiencies
- Warehousing systems
- Capital commitments
- Supplier reliability
- Make-or-buy options

Inventories
- Supplier capabilities
- Just-in-time procedures
- Purchasing practices
- Carrying costs
- Production planning
- Distribution capabilities
- Customer loyalty
- Out-of-stock risks
- Obsolescence threats

Intangibles
- Brand management
- Service contracts
- Support and service requirements
- Systems capabilities

Payables and Accruals
- Supplier base and purchasing power
- Payment policies
- Discounts and allowances
- Credit availability

Application to Fair Values under the Cost Approach

In valuing a reporting or cash-generating unit, it may be misleading to rely on the return on capital calculated under GAAP or IFRS, which is based on the book values of the operating assets. The DuPont analysis is useful to management when assessing a reporting or cash-generating unit against guideline entities.

The technique can supply practical support to value conclusions from the replacement cost method by demonstrating that the returns on the adjusted equity are reasonable in relation to the risks involved. The formulas for determining some standard parameters in applying the DuPont analysis to values obtained by the cost approach are shown here.

$$\text{Return on Equity} = \frac{\text{Pretax Return} \times \text{Asset Turnover}}{\text{Leverage Ratio}}$$

$$\text{Pretax Return} = \frac{\text{Earnings Before Taxes}}{\text{Total Assets at Replacement Cost}}$$

$$\text{Total Assets} = \text{Financial} + \text{Physical} + \text{Going-Concern Component} + \text{Effective Goodwill}$$

$$\text{Leverage Ratio} = \frac{\text{Equity at Replacement Cost}}{\text{Total Assets at Replacement Cost}}$$

As discussed in Chapter 5, "Projecting What Is to Come," most firms have vats of red ink hidden away. According to *Islands of Profit in a Sea of Red Ink*, by Jonathan Byrnes (Portfolio, 2011), at least 35% of every company's business, by account, product, transaction, or any other measure, is unprofitable. That situation is disguised by the fact that more than 20% of the business is sufficiently profitable to cross-subsidize the losses.

Managements are always concerned with profitability. For a reporting or cash-generating unit, Byrnes's process starts with a profit map (not the same as a value map) showing where, at around 70% accuracy, the firm is making or losing money. According to Byrnes:

> When you do this, you can create a very powerful, detailed analysis of your company. You can see your company's profitability, customer by customer, and product by product. . . . Importantly, you can easily project the impact of changing your mix of customers and products, and you can see the impact of changing your costs in a set of highly targeted initiatives.

Byrnes suggests that the initial action should be to secure the high-profit segments of the business and determine how best to expand them. Only then should management turn to shutting off the red ink by developing processes to improve the marginal parts, which almost always have champions. Getting beyond that primarily psychological barrier starts with accepting the concept that gardeners prune the branches of trees and bushes to help them reach their full potential. Those needing heavy pruning fall into three categories:

1. *Healthy branches that aren't the best.* Good gardeners constantly examine trees and bushes to see which parts are worthy of the plant's limited strength, and cut off the rest. Jack Welch, the former CEO of General Electric, did that when he declared that any of the company's businesses that could not be No. 1 or No. 2 in its field would be sold.
2. *Sick branches that won't recover.* At some point, a gardener realizes that more water, fertilizer, and hope won't help. Welch followed that logic when he declared that any GE business that was struggling—in effect, sick—would be fixed, closed, or sold, and that the bottom 10% of the workforce would be let go each year.
3. *Dead branches that take up space.* Anything dead takes up space. Welch was celebrated for trying to get rid of layers of bureaucracy to improve communications, productivity, and the flow of ideas.

Before taking such actions, managers should consider their intellectual and emotional responses: Is pruning appealing? Does it make your stomach queasy? Business success requires embracing the premise that pruning is necessary, natural, and beneficial. Endings and new beginnings are linked—you can't have one without the other.

CHAPTER TEN

Sources of Value—Risks

Let everyone have confidence in the future.

—*Wen Jiabao (1942–), Chinese premier and statesman*

C HAPTER 9 STATED THAT there are only two means to increase the value of an enterprise—increase profits or reduce risks. It went on to discuss some ways of improving profits: innovation, value maps, DuPont analyses, and elimination of loss-making areas. In the simplest of terms, the value of an entity is its net income divided by an appropriate capitalization rate; the first way of increasing value has two beneficial effects. It raises the numerator (net income) and, by adding growth, reduces the denominator (capitalization rate). This chapter deals with the other side of the equation, the reduction of risks, defined by the *Oxford English Dictionary* as:

> Exposure to the possibility of loss, injury, or other adverse or unwel-come circumstance; a chance or situation involving such possibility.

With respect to businesses, the most common risks are listed as factors in developing capitalization rates by a buildup method (see Chapter 8).

REDUCING RISKS

The first and easiest way to reduce risks in a firm is to improve the quality of its employees and their interactions. A contentious but effective method is to use intelligence quotient (IQ) tests, which have been shown to measure more than quick-wittedness, as part of the hiring procedures. They were first put forward over 100 years ago, by the British psychologist Charles Spearman, who claimed that test results were dependent on an individual's general cognitive ability, g. While particular tests might measure other factors as well, g was the key underlying ingredient.

Opponents have for years said that various IQ tests measure different things, and that success is determined not by an underlying common factor but by how well individuals' abilities in specific areas match the challenges they face. They are wrong, claim three American psychologists, Nathan Kuncel and Sarah Hezlett of the University of Illinois and Deniz Ones of the University of Minnesota. This group asserts that general cognitive ability exists and "predicts a broad spectrum of important life outcomes, including academic achievement, health-related behaviors, social outcomes, job performance, and creativity, among many others."

In support of this conclusion, they reviewed 127 studies involving 20,352 subjects over many years. They focused on the Miller Analogies Test (MAT), which is not simply a test of IQ, but requires a combination of knowledge and reasoning ability. Participants are given three words and asked to find a fourth that fits the other three by analogy. Tests typically involve 100 questions with a half minute allowed for each, to choose from a menu of four alternatives. Those scoring highly on the MAT also tend to do well in the jobs they choose and are more highly rated by their employers. The correlations were as high for work measurements as they were for academic ones. Therefore, one way of reducing risks may be to concentrate on hiring candidates with high IQs.

 CONTINUAL MONITORING AND TESTING

Many managers consider that the volume and complexity of risks faced by organizations today are at an all-time high. To get a sense for the extent of those involved, researchers into enterprise risk management at North Carolina State University in 2010 asked a number of respondents to describe the extent to which the volume and complexity of risks they face have increased in the past five years. Sixteen percent reported "a great deal," while 46% responded "extensively;" only 2% indicated no change at all.

Those increases have had major effects on the organizations surveyed. Just over 6% of respondents noted that their companies were impacted by operational surprises "a great deal;" an additional 30% replied "extensively," and 33% responded "moderately." The total of these responses (69%) was slightly higher than the proportion that reported suffering from a greater volume and complexity of risks (62%). For many, increased risks are creating significant operational issues not anticipated by managements.

In any business, one well-established way to reduce risks is to improve the internal controls intended to manage them; it is essential that all activities are continually monitored and tested by the firm's Internal Control over Financial Reporting (ICFR) staff and auditors. As well as strong internal controls, it is essential to have appropriate, extensive, and often rigorous governance practices. However, as we observe in everyday life, human biases can undermine judgment, leading to regrettable choices. Governance processes typically do not fully take into account these biases, which can result in errors that grievously impact the value of a firm.

Peter Drucker, the Austrian-born economist who was one of the founders of effective organizational management in the United States, observed that "most discussions of decision making assume that only senior executives make decisions, or that only senior executives' decisions matter. This is a dangerous mistake." This conclusion seems to be true for more than companies; research suggests that all of us need to look within ourselves and examine our inherent biases, which can hinder sound judgments. Those leaders and managers who recognize these biases may find a *judgment framework* helpful. This is a set of principles encouraging critical and good-faith thought processes, to enable decision makers to consider situations more holistically and derive more consistent results.

At its core, judgment is not formulaic; no framework will result in consistently correct and effective decisions. However, analogous frameworks are used in other professions for similar purposes. In most English-speaking countries, laws are generally applied through *legal doctrines*. Those are frameworks of procedures, steps, and tests, often established by precedents, through which judgments can be determined in a given set of circumstances. A doctrine comes about when a judge makes a ruling in which a process is sufficiently outlined and applied that it becomes equally useful in similar situations.

To understand the biases that we all carry around, it is important to know that we make decisions in two ways. The first is an intuitive gut feeling, which works quickly and instinctively, sometimes as merely an emotional reaction. The second is more analytic, holistic, and thoughtful. In today's fast and competitive world, most of us find ourselves under the gun, often jumping to conclusions rather than gathering the relevant data and considering alternatives.

An excellent example of a fundamental change in decision making comes from professional sports. In *Judgment in Managerial Decision Making* (John Wiley & Sons, 7th ed., 2008), Max Bazerman describes how Billy Beane, as manager of the Oakland Athletics, transformed team building in baseball from an exercise in intuition to a highly analytic process by establishing which statistics actually predicted future runs scored. This led his team to enormous success with a significantly lower payroll than its major league competitors. Other baseball executives seem to have been guilty of (1) generalizing from personal experience, (2) putting excessive emphasis on most recent performance, and (3) ranking what they saw above statistical data; in short, their decisions were biased.

DEALING WITH BIASES

While we all have biases, asking the following questions can offset some of the most common ones:

- *Do we have all the facts?* Often gut decisions are made with insufficient facts and too many hunches. As part of gathering and evaluating facts, assess their stability. Are they likely to change during the course of this transaction or in its aftermath?
- *What are the business reasons or substance of the transaction?* Without this knowledge any decision is likely to be flawed.
- *Is there another point of view?* An outsider's perspective can uncover biases and reduce overconfidence.
- *What are the possible alternatives?* Considering alternatives simultaneously, as opposed to sequentially, reduces the susceptibility to reliance on recently learned information. Weighing choices separately rather than jointly results in more likelihood of bias.
- *Does the opposite position have merit?* This reduces overconfidence and helps avoid gut-based rather more logical, fact-oriented decisions.
- *Should the decision be made by a group of designated experts?* Up to three collaborators increase decision-making accuracy significantly; more provide only small improvements.

RISK RATE COMPONENT MODEL

Since 1991, a well-established means of assessing the risks of a firm is the Risk Rate Component Model (RRCM). This uses a system of ratio and other comparative analyses to assist management in discovering both the risks and the rewards of individual small or medium-sized enterprises (SMEs) and thus to arrive at a reasonable cost of equity not based on rates of return for public companies.

It begins with a so-called risk-free rate, typically the yield on 10-year government bonds, to which it adds four separate premiums covering the risks associated with competition, financial strength, management ability and depth, and profitability and stability of earnings (see Table 10.1). It makes further adjustments to reflect the impact of national or local economic circumstances. The four categories represent material and significant aspects of a business, with each being ranked on a scale of 0 (none) to 10 (high). The material in this section is drawn, with permission, from the chapter "Risks and Rewards" by William A. Hanlin Jr. and J. Richard Claywell, two of my fellow directors of the International Association of Consultants, Valuators, and Analysts (IACVA), in my previous book, *Guide to Fair Value under IFRS* (John Wiley & Sons, 2010).

Assuming a risk-free rate of 5%, the RRCM will develop a cost of equity ranging from a low of 1% (5% + 0% + 0% + 0% + 0% − 2% − 2%) to a high of 49% (5% + 10% + 10% + 10% + 10% + 2% + 2%). Reducing any of the perceived risks will lower the cost of equity and increase the fair value of the firm.

TABLE 10.1 Summary of Premiums for the RRCM

Category	High	Medium High	Average	Medium Low	Low	No Risk
Competition	10	7.5	5	2.5	1	0
Financial strength	10	7.5	5	2.5	1	0
Management ability & depth	10	7.5	5	2.5	1	0
Profitability & stability of earnings	10	7.5	5	2.5	1	0

Economic Conditions	Weak	Medium Weak	Neutral	Medium Strong	Strong
National	Add 2	Add 1	0	Less 1	Less 2
Local or regional	Add 2	Add 1	0	Less 1	Less 2

Competition

Table 10.2 illustrates how a hypothetical firm, Moloch Inc., might be graded in the competition category.

Proprietary Content

Risks associated with proprietary content are assessed by reviewing the relevant documents, the time remaining in any protection period, and the importance placed by management on its contribution to the success of the business. In this case, a more efficient process gives the firm significant advantages by lowering the cost of sales.

Relative Size

The relative size indicator compares Moloch's revenue to that of the entire relevant market to give an indication of the comparative risk. For instance, a local hardware store may operate a single location; its size (and therefore risk) is measured against the revenues, asset size, and number of employees for all such stores in the appropriate geographic and demographic areas. Conclusion: Small is bad!

TABLE 10.2 Moloch Inc. RRCM Competition Grading

Indicator	Risk Level	Weight	Weighted Risk Factor
Proprietary content (including patents and copyrights)	1.5	2	3
Relative size of company	7.5	2	15
Relative product or service quality	5.0	2	10
Product or service differentiation	2.5	2	5
Covenant not to compete	1.0	2	2
Market strength—competition	6.0	2	12
Market size/share	8.0	2	16
Price competition	3.5	2	7
Ease of entry	5.0	2	10
Other	0.0	0	0
Total weight factors		18	80
Weighted average premium			4.4

Relative Product or Service Quality

Quality is analyzed by comparing Moloch's products or services to those offered by competitors. How do they differ from others in the industry? If they are the same, then a figure of 5.0 would be assigned as an average risk; if better, a lower figure is applicable.

Product or Service Differentiation

Assessing differences involves many considerations: How many competitors are there? What factors affect customer buying patterns (timing, seasonal, etc.)? Are substitute products or services available? How important are pricing, name recognition, use of technical know-how, customer loyalty, licensing restrictions, and so forth?

Covenant to Not Compete

All key personnel should have employment agreements containing nondisclosure provisions and a covenant to not compete for a reasonable period after employment ceases. Management should review the terms of all such agreements, including expiry date, territory covered, likelihood of competition, and so on.

Market Strength

Market strength is a measure of lower risks associated with longevity, reputation, customer care, and so forth, and depends on which portion of a market the firm serves. There is usually only average risk in a business with a lot of small competitors, such as auto repair. However, high risks may occur in industries with a few large competitors if one dominates due to technology, size, or innovation.

Price Competition

Customer price sensitivity is a major factor in higher or lower risks. It may be measured by comparable profit margins subject to pressure from competitors that are able to offer products or provide services at significantly lower prices.

Ease of Entry

Ease of entry measures the ability of a new competitor to enter the market. For example, an established dentist in any community will surely see new competitors from time to time, but the newcomers have significant costs to enter the business—education, equipment, premises, marketing, and so on.

Financial

The subject's normal financial ratios are the basis for most of those risk factors; some also require a comparison to the industry. In most developed economies, such data is available; in the United States, the major sources are Risk Management Associates (RMA), which draws its data from banks, and MicroBit Corporation's Integra Benchmarking Data. Ideally, management will compare the financial ratios of the firm with those of comparable entities in their local economies. If, due to lack of data, this is impractical, the easily available U.S. databases, although they are not specifically relevant, allow a benchmark comparison between Moloch and businesses in an established economy that can be modified on a global basis.

Table 10.3 shows how Moloch might be graded for financial strength.

TABLE 10.3   Moloch Inc. RRCM Financial Strength Grading

Indicator	Risk Level	Weight	Weighted Risk
Level of Liquidity			
Current ratio	2	3	6
Quick ratio	5	2	10
Sales to working capital	3.5	2	7
Quality of Liquidity			
Receivables to working capital	5	2	10
Inventory to working capital	6	2	12
Asset Utilization			
Net sales to inventory turnover	7.5	2	15
Total assets to sales	5	2	10
Net fixed assets to equity	7.5	2	15
Miscellaneous assets to equity	2.5	1	2.5
Leverage Ratios			
Total debt to equity	5	2	10
Equity multiplier (total assets to equity)	6	2	12
Total debt to assets	5	3	15
			(continued)

TABLE 10.3 *(Continued)*

Indicator	Risk Level	Weight	Weighted Risk
Long-term debt to equity	5	3	15
Interest coverage	5	2	10
Total weight factors		30	149.5
Weighted average premium			5

Management

The first five indicators in Table 10.4 are calculated from the financial records to assess management's abilities. When the data is available, the indicators should be compared to industry averages, as the intention is to determine the relative risks of Moloch through comparisons with other participants. A manufacturer turns over its inventory 4.1 times a year; is this high or low? The answer lies in the question, "Is it similar to, slower than, or faster than the industry norm?" A good way of assessing management depth is to investigate the entity's operational structure. In situations where the owner is dominant, with no one else allowed to make any important commitments, the risks are much higher than in one with several trained staff accustomed to making decisions.

Table 10.4 shows how Moloch might be graded for management ability and depth.

TABLE 10.4 Moloch Inc. RRCM Management Ability and Depth Grading

Indicator	Risk Level	Weight	Weighted Risk
Accounts receivable turnover—days	7.0	2.0	14.0
Accounts payable turnover—days	7.0	2.0	14.0
Inventory turnover—days	5.0	2.0	10.0
Fixed asset turnover	5.0	2.0	10.0
Employee turnover	2.0	2.0	4.0
Management depth	5.0	2.0	10.0
Facilities involvement	5.0	2.0	10.0
Family involvement	0.0	0.0	0.0

(continued)

TABLE 10.4   *(Continued)*

Indicator	Risk Level	Weight	Weighted Risk
Books and records—quality and history	5.0	2.0	10.0
Contracts	5.0	2.0	10.0
Gross margin	5.0	2.0	10.0
Operating margin	5.0	2.0	10.0
Operating cycle	5.0	2.0	10.0
Other	0.0	0.0	0.0
Total weight factors		24.0	122.0
Weighted average premium			5.1

Profitability

Table 10.5 shows how Moloch might rank in profitability and stability of earnings.

Altman Z-Score

All of the measures in Table 10.5 are well known, except for the Altman Z-score. This is a common method of estimating the likelihood of a firm becoming bankrupt and is found to be accurate over 70% of the time. It is important to understand that all changes to the Z-score, as well as its level, must be monitored; a business whose score dropped from 2.80 to 1.95 in a single year would be of

TABLE 10.5   Moloch Inc. RRCM Management Profitability and Statement of Earnings Grading

Indicator	Risk Level	Weight	Weighted Risk
Time in business	7.0	2.0	14.0
Industry life cycle	5.0	2.0	10.0
Return on sales (before taxes)	2.5	2.0	5.0
Return on equity	8.5	3.0	25.5
Return on assets	2.5	3.0	7.5
Trading ratio	5.0	2.0	10.0

(continued)

TABLE 10.5 *(Continued)*

Indicator	Risk Level	Weight	Weighted Risk
Operating earnings growth rate	5.0	2.0	10.0
Sales growth rate	5.0	2.0	10.0
Standard deviation of earnings	8.5	2.0	17.0
Altman Z-score	2.0	2.0	4.0
Other	0.0	0.0	0.0
Total weight factors		22.0	113.0
Weighted average premium			5.1

greater concern than one that had remained between 1.70 and 1.85 for five years. The Z-score may be regarded as an early warning system, which balances and puts into perspective five financial indicators. The calculation is as follows:

$$Z = 0.012X(1) + 0.014X(2) + 0.033X(3) + 0.006X(4) + 0.999X(5)$$

where

$X(1)$ = Working Capital/Total Assets
$X(2)$ = Retained Earnings/Total Assets
$X(3)$ = Earnings before Interest and Taxes/Total Assets
$X(4)$ = Total Equity/Total Debt
$X(5)$ = Sales/Total Assets

Note: Variables $X(1)$ to $X(4)$ are converted from percentages as whole numbers, while $X(5)$ is converted to a decimal. If $X(1) = 15.5\%$, it is recorded as 15.5, not 0.155; if $X(5)$ is 95%, it becomes 0.95.

Moloch has the following ratios:

$X(1)$ = −20.3%
$X(2)$ = −15%
$X(3)$ = −9.4%
$X(4)$ = −5.2%
$X(5)$ = 118%

Thus,

$$Z = (0.012)(-20.3) + (0.014)(-15) + (0.033)(-9.4) + (0.006)(-5.2) + (0.999)(1.18)$$

$$= -0.2436 - 0.2100 - 0.3102 - .0312 + 1.1788$$
$$= 0.03838 \text{ or } 3.84\%$$

Z-Score Significance

Range	Chance of Failure
1.80% or less	Very high
1.81% to 2.70%	High
2.71% to 2.90%	Possible
2.91% or higher	Not likely

Other Risks

Other items to be considered when using the RRCM are the effects of regional and national economic outlooks. To utilize the technique successfully requires a working knowledge of ratio analyses. The model uses entity-specific qualitative and quantitative factors to estimate a reasonable cost of equity and allow managers to understand the factors influencing fair value.

 INTELLECTUAL CAPITAL VALUE DRIVERS

Today, many businesses are knowledge-intensive, with much of their value hidden in people's heads, computer systems, processes, relationships, and networks, as discussed in Chapters 6, 7, and 8. The main valuation approaches emphasize cash flows, not assets. They start with the income statement and pay little attention to the balance sheet, making extensive assumptions about the intangible "factory" behind the cash flows. To maximize performance and valuation in today's business, management also needs to focus on the intangible assets that make up a firm's intellectual capital (IC).

Trek Consulting Inc. of Boston has developed the "IC Value Drivers Report," an innovative technique that measures the hidden, intangible drivers of performance and value in the following 10 categories: management, employees, processes/information technology (IT), marketing/sales, technology/

intellectual property, customers, network, reputation/brand, business model, and external factors. The data comes from structured crowd-sourcing, including interviews with internal and external stakeholders using a proprietary, standardized assessment tool designed to measure the value and growth drivers of middle market companies. This was developed based on the experience of Trek's principals, as well as input from industry experts. The objective is to rate the strength of an organization's IC value drivers. Those ratings can be converted into a road map to a higher fair value. The rating scale is from 1.0 (low) to 5.0 (high):

Best	4.5 to 5.0
Above average	3.5 to 4.4
Average	2.5 to 3.4
Below average	1.5 to 2.4
Worst	1.0 to 1.4

During the interviews, Trek personnel also solicit comments about the thinking behind the responses about specific matters, as well as general questions about the outlook for the company and possible opportunities for growth.

 ## CONCLUSION

The chapter has described some of the ways a firm can increase its fair value by reducing the risks that have to be reflected in its capitalization or discount rates. While less glamorous than accentuating growth through innovation or the elimination of loss-making activities, such achievements are an essential part of improving values.

CHAPTER ELEVEN

Valuing Liabilities

If only people who worry about their liabilities
would think about the riches they do possess,
they would stop worrying.

—Dale Carnegie (1888–1955), American author

S O FAR, WE HAVE DEALT MAINLY with valuing assets because most investors relate to those items. However, fair value also applies to liabilities, especially in purchase price allocations (PPAs—see Chapter 13). In effect, liabilities are valued as assets to their counterparties (owners/lenders), often generating counterintuitive results. As an entity's credit rating declines, the fair value of its liabilities decreases, giving rise to imaginary gains that are reported through other comprehensive income (OCI). Credit ratings are important indicators of the major risks relating to liabilities—that the entity will default or otherwise fail to perform its obligations as they come due. Another significant factor affecting the value of a liability is the existence of embedded derivatives, such as rights to convert into equity.

LIABILITIES TRANSFERRED RATHER THAN SETTLED

Since the Financial Accounting Standards Board (FASB) issued the Statement of Financial Accounting Standards (SFAS) 157 in 2006, Generally Accepted Accounting Principles (GAAP) has valued liabilities on a transfer basis; however, the International Accounting Standards Board (IASB) did not always agree. As recently as a 2010 exposure draft of a new International Financial Reporting Standard (IFRS) to replace International Accounting Standard (IAS) 37, *Provisions, Contingent Liabilities and Contingent Assets*, it emphasized that liabilities should not be measured at hypothetical transfer or cancellation prices. However, the standards define the fair value of a liability as the amount that would be paid to transfer the obligation to a market participant at the measurement date, with the liability to the counterparty (lender) continuing, rather than being settled, and with the nonperformance risk remaining the same. Consequently, the fair value of a liability must take into account all nonperformance risk, including the entity's own credit standing. How management intends to settle it, or the amount that might be paid to the counterparty for extinguishment, has no influence on the fair value, which reflects only market participants' estimate of the discounted future cash outflows, adjusted for uncertainty.

Transfers of liabilities are rare; in practice, most are settled with the holder or extinguished through an offsetting contract; therefore, measuring their fair values is a challenge. FASB and IASB concluded that settlement is an entity-specific decision, and the difference between the settlement amount and fair value is an element of performance. Among the differences is the impact of credit risk, which is not usually considered in settlement. However, a firm that is a potential purchaser, as an asset, of an obligation of another entity, will always take into account the strength of the issuer's credit in determining the amount it is willing to pay.

Market Participant Assumptions

The fair value of a liability reflects assumptions that a market participant would use to establish a purchase price, including all inherent risks. This is most easily done by considering the amount the existing owner could receive through its sale as a financial asset. A measurement (for example, "marked to model") that does not include an adjustment for nonperformance risk is not fair value. Every such calculation should include an amount market participants would demand due to the risks (uncertainties) inherent in a particular valuation technique, as well as in the relevant inputs; determining the appropriate adjustment can be complex.

One practical expedient is to look at comparable entities with publicly traded debt securities as a source of market participants' views. Another alternative is to adopt common industry conventions (e.g., quoted default rates to establish credit reserves and WACC as the discount rate) if they appear consistent with the expectations of market participants. History and past transactions may help to determine how effective management has been at dealing with credit contractions.

Nonperformance Risks

Credit risk, a major component of nonperformance risk, will vary among an entity's liabilities, depending on their term and nature. For example, the credit risk of payables or other current items is likely to be lower than that for longer-term, unsecured liabilities, but higher than that for a long-term debt such as a mortgage; the greatest risks relate to junior, subordinate, unsecured notes. It is important to investigate the obligations of all component legal entities, which in the event of liquidation, may effectively have a higher priority against key assets, than the parent's claim.

An entity's credit rating (say BBB) is not necessarily equivalent to the effects of credit risks on the fair values of its liabilities. As shown by the prices of traded credit default swaps, a form of liability insurance that pays off in the event of default, such spreads often fluctuate based on sentiment, without any change in the borrower's credit rating. Nonperformance risks also consider any collateral or credit enhancements involved, such as third-party guarantees. For a third-party guarantee to affect the fair value of a liability, it must be an attribute of the instrument and inseparable from it. If the guarantee is payable directly to the holder and not to the issuer, in the FASB's and IASB's view it is not part of the liability itself but a separate instrument and therefore irrelevant to the fair value.

Other Factors to Consider

In many cases, a bank may be willing to assume term deposit liabilities for less than their principal amount because, for example, of their relatively low funding cost. In effect, the difference is the cost of purchasing offsetting intangible asset "core deposits." These are amortized, as additional interest, over the lives of the related liabilities. Certain obligations, such as those relating to asbestos damages or performance guarantees, have uncertainties about both the amounts and the timing of the ultimate payments. The party assuming such liabilities will have costs to manage them and probably require a profit.

The entity should try to anticipate the impact, in the form of additional yield, that a market participant would require for all risks, including those previously discussed, affecting the value of a liability. Often this involves the use of market-based credit spreads (i.e., the difference between yields on Treasury securities and traded obligations of a similar term, with different quality ratings). It is important to understand the unique nature of each individual liability in determining the appropriate level of credit and other risks, such as lack of marketability.

Settlement Amount versus Fair Value

The fair value of a liability is determined under the transfer concept, which includes nonperformance risk; there is no exemption or practical expedient. The basic premise is that the liability lives on until maturity. Any difference between fair value and the settlement amount is not recognized until extinguishment.

Example

A $1,000,000 note is due by Gamma Corporation to Mutual Bank. It has a market value of only $950,000 from the risk of nonperformance, as economic conditions in the borrower's industry have deteriorated. On settlement, Gamma would be required to pay the face amount to be relieved of the obligation, as Mutual Bank, with full knowledge of its actual financial condition, is unlikely to be willing to discount the note except under exceptional circumstances.

To calculate the transfer value, Gamma must construct a hypothetical transaction in which another party (Delta Inc.), with a similar credit profile, is seeking financing on terms substantially the same as the note. Delta could choose either (1) to enter into a new loan agreement with a bank on terms that reflect the industry's situation, such as 25 bp higher interest, or (2) to receive cash on a transfer of the note from Gamma. In this hypothetical transaction, as the present value of the net cash flows, discounted at its cost of borrowing, is the same, Delta should be indifferent to how it obtains the financing. Therefore, the transfer amount (fair value), reflecting the market participants' views of the industry's credit risk, would be $950,000, the market value, $50,000 less than the settlement amount. ■

Impact of Credit Changes

The fact that nonperformance risk is reflected in the fair values of an entity's liabilities means that its impact will be the opposite of its financial situation. Deterioration of the entity's credit standing results in a higher discount rate for the future cash flows associated with a liability. This will result in a reduction of its fair value, creating a reported gain in the income statement; conversely an improvement in the credit standing will result in a lower discount rate, higher fair value of the liabilities, and a reported loss.

Calculation of Debenture Values

Now we move from the theoretical to the practical. This example deals with estimates in April 2011 of the fair values of two series of *pari passu* (ranking equally), secured debentures of Omega Mining Corporation. They were both issued on April 9, 2009, just after the bottom of the stock market collapse (though of course, management did not recognize it), with five-year terms to mature in 2014. The Series B issue bore interest at 10%; Series C, with interest at 5%, was convertible into common shares. If these rates seem high, consider that in late 2008, Goldman Sachs Group Inc. raised $5 billion in preferred shares at 10% with warrants to buy common shares attached.

From 2009 to 2011, the common shares of Omega increased 174% from $9.06 to $24.83 as the firm generated significant profits. As a result, the company's credit spread over U.S. Treasuries has, in the view of market participants, declined by 70%, from 8.13% to 2.41%, as demonstrated by a recent new issue of 10-year, 6% Series D debentures:

	Series B	Series D
	April 2009	April 2011
5-year Treasury note	1.87%	—
10-year Treasury bond	—	3.59%
Omega borrowing cost spread	8.13%	2.41%
Yield on issuance	10.00%	6.00%

Series B Debentures

The market-driven credit spread and the current three-year Treasury note rate give an estimated borrowing cost in April 2011 for the Series B debentures:

Three-year Treasury rate	1.34%
Market spread	2.41%
Three-year Omega borrowing cost	3.75%

Table 11.1 shows the present values at 3.75% (Omega's current three-year borrowing cost) of the cash outflows to Omega and inflows to investors.

Series C Debentures

The Series C debentures consist of two elements, a bond that would be valued in the same way as the Series B and an embedded derivative that represents the right, but not an obligation, to convert each $1,000 debenture into 85 common shares at $11.76 each. This was a 30% premium to the average closing price of $9.06 for the 10 trading days (two weeks) before the issue was priced in April 2009 (see Table 11.2).

The value to an investor of the Series C debentures on issuance would have only been $816.62 per $1,000 face amount, the balance of $183.38 being represented by the conversion rights into 85 shares, ascribed at $2.157 each.

Values of Conversion Rights

The value of an option, such as the Series C conversion rights, is usually calculated by an option pricing model. The most common is the Black-Scholes

TABLE 11.1   Omega Mining 2011 Value of Series B Debentures

Date		Payment per $1,000 Debenture 10.00% ($)	Present Value Factor 3.75%	Present Value ($)
2011	October	50	0.9816	49.08
2012	April	50	0.9639	48.19
	October	50	0.9461	47.31
2013	April	50	0.9290	46.45
	October	50	0.9119	45.60
2014	April	1,050	0.8954	940.21
				1,176.84
Present Values as % of Face Amount				117.68
Market Participant Profit (1% per year)				(3.53)
Fair Value as % of Face Amount				114.15

TABLE 11.2 Omega Mining 2009 Value of Series C Debentures

Date		Payment per $1,000 Debenture 5.00% ($)	Present Value Factor 10.00%	Present Value ($)
2009	October	25	0.9524	23.81
2010	April	25	0.9091	22.73
	October	25	0.8658	21.65
2011	April	25	0.8264	20.66
	October	25	0.8112	20.28
2012	April	25	0.7513	18.78
	October	25	0.7375	18.44
2013	April	25	0.6830	17.08
	October	25	0.6704	16.76
2014	April	1,025	0.6209	636.44
				816.62
Conversion right				183.38
Face amount				1,000.00

model (BSM), found on several websites. It needs only the six parameters listed in Table 11.3.

Expected Volatility

Most readers will be familiar with all the inputs except for expected volatility. The volatility of a share's price is the rate and magnitude of its previous changes, both up and down; it is usually calculated by the standard deviation of their dispersion using daily or weekly data over a period similar to that of the option.

The BSM requires a figure for expected volatility; this is the past volatility adjusted for current and anticipated conditions. For Omega, the actual volatility for the five years up to the debenture issuances was 33%. That figure was far lower than that for the previous 12 months, which had risen to 75%, due to the share price collapsing in 2008 and 2009. In fact, the issuance was just after the bottom of the stock market decline, although at the time virtually no one believed in a fast recovery. Therefore, the investment banker pricing the deal used 54% (the mean) as the anticipated volatility.

By 2011, markets had become more stable, the share price had risen significantly, and the volatility had declined naturally to 23% for the past three

TABLE 11.3 Omega Mining Value of Conversion Rights

	April 2009 Issue	April 2011 Valuation
Share price	$9.06	$24.83
Exercise price	$11.76	$11.76
Risk-free rate	1.87%	1.34%
Anticipated dividend yield	0.00%	0.00%
Anticipated life	5.0 years	3.0 years
Expected volatility	54%	28%
Value of each option	$3.66	$14.53

years. However, with uncertainties in the prices of many of the metals mined by Omega, the valuator decided to use 28%, the average between the pre-crisis level and the current level (33% and 23% respectively) as the expected volatility.

The conclusions are that on issuance, the conversion options were actually worth $3.70, equivalent to $314.50 per $1,000 debenture. This is 71.5% above the ascribed amount. The latter figure of $2.57 indicated an expected volatility of 34% (around the pre-crisis rate). In 2011, the options are worth $14.53 each.

Value of Series C Debentures in 2011

Table 11.4 calculates the value of the Series C debentures without any conversion rights is now $1,122.29 per $1,000 unit.

TABLE 11.4 Omega Mining 2011 Value of Series C Debentures

Date		Payment per $1,000 Debenture 5.00% $	Present Value Factor 3.75%	Present Value $
2011	October	1,025	0.9816	1,006.13
2012	April	25	0.9639	24.10
	October	25	0.9461	23.65
2013	April	25	0.9290	23.23
	October	25	0.9119	22.80
2014	April	25	0.8954	22.39
				1,122.29

To this amount must be added the value ($1,234.99) of 85 options at $14.53 each for a total of $2,357.28; this is 11.7% greater than the amount ($2,110.55) obtained on full conversion ($24.83 multiplied by 85); the 11.7% premium represents the investor's return for waiting:

Fair value without conversion rights	$1,122.29
Fair value of conversion rights	$1,234.99
Total	$2,357.28
Converted value market price	$2,110.55
Premium over converted value	11.7%

As with the Series B debentures, market participants would want a profit for accepting the transfer; using the same 3% gives a fair value of $2,287 ($2,357.28 times 0.97) per $1,000 debenture. For accounting purposes, the premium of $1,287 is amortized over the remaining three-year term as an offset to interest paid.

 ## ASSET RETIREMENT OBLIGATIONS

Many organizations are subject to legal requirements associated with the retirement of long-lived physical assets. Every entity so affected must recognize the fair value of an asset retirement obligation (ARO) in the period in which it is incurred, unless the amount cannot yet be reasonably estimated. It represents the payment that a willing third party of comparable credit standing would demand to assume all of the duties, uncertainties, and risks inherent in the ARO. The fair value of this liability is calculated under the fair value framework discussed in Chapter 3.

Unit of Account

The unit of account is the total legal obligation on retirement of the asset. The ARO is recorded at fair value in the first year that the requirements of GAAP or IFRS are met. When a new ARO layer is established, due to a change in the timing or amount of expected cash flows, it is treated as a separate unit of account.

Valuation Premise

No valuation premise is applicable to liabilities, as fair value assumes they are transferred to a market participant.

Principal Market

There is unlikely to be a principal market for an ARO, as they are not actively traded and there is little or no observable data on the prices paid to transfer them.

Most Advantageous Market

The most advantageous market is the one in which the minimal amount is paid to transfer the ARO; management generally develops a hypothetical market.

Valuation Methods

All three valuation approaches methods must be considered. Quoted prices in active markets are used if available; however, an expected present value technique is the usual default.

- ▩ *Market approach.* What information from market transactions involving comparable items is publicly available?
- ▩ *Income approach.* Is there data to develop discounted cash flows projections using market participants' inputs?
- ▩ *Cost approach.* Can an estimate of the amount required to do the necessary remediation work be reliably established?

 ## CONTINGENT LIABILITIES

Under IFRS, contingent liabilities are dealt with by a special standard, IAS 37, *Provisions, Contingent Liabilities and Contingent Assets.* Under GAAP, they are covered by SFAS 5, *Accounting for Contingencies.* Since 2002, IASB has been trying to develop a new IFRS dealing with the subject, and in 2005 issued an exposure draft. There are significant problems in valuing individual provisions, which are "liabilities of uncertain timing or amount," or contingent liabilities, which are "possible obligations" arising from past events and whose existence will be confirmed in the future.

In general, provisions are shown in financial statements, and contingent liabilities, which often relate to litigation, are disclosed only in the notes. Accountants tend to be very conservative; an old adage is "When in doubt, book the liability." However, this is not the case for contingencies; therefore, it is necessary to read the notes carefully before investing or lending money. Sometimes significant risks are not recorded, as they are neither "probable" nor "reasonably estimable." There may also be remote risks, like early-stage legal claims that do not need to be disclosed.

Warranty Costs

Product warranties, a virtually universal service, are assumed to give rise to probable liabilities that can be reasonably estimated. When goods are sold, an estimate of the amount of warranty costs likely to be incurred is recorded as an expense. In effect, the liability is measured by the cost approach.

Many costs are similar to warranties. Companies may offer coupons, prizes, rebates, air miles, free hotel stays, free rentals, and similar items associated with sales activity. Each gives rise to an estimated liability. While the details may vary, the basic procedures and outcomes are similar.

Environmental Obligations

When considering acquisitions of physical assets, great care must be taken to ascertain that they are clean, particularly when the present or a previous owner has handled toxic materials on the site. The acquirer must assess the probability, timing, and quantum of costs that may be incurred to correct environmental problems, past, current, or future, ensuring compliance with all relevant legislation and regulations on an ongoing basis. Situations exist where the value of a business was virtually erased by the costs of cleaning up a location. While large profits had previously been earned from the plant, the acquirer inherited the complete environmental liability and became responsible for cleaning up the unfortunate contamination from an owner well back in the chain of title.

In many jurisdictions, environmental legislation is far-reaching and often based on the "deep pockets" theory, whereby the one with the most resources pays for cleanup and reclamation. While auditors are not required to express an opinion on the adequacy of an entity's environmental practices or compliance with pertinent laws and regulations, they must obtain sufficient evidence to provide reasonable assurance that any items on the financial statements that could be affected by environmental considerations are fairly presented. Although this gives no assurance that the costs of a cleanup have been fully taken into account, it should be the starting point for the assessment of this type of exposure. In certain cases, a consulting engineer or environmental specialist may be necessary.

The accounting profession has difficulty with risks that have not yet crystallized and may never do so. In valuing a reporting or cash-generating unit, it is nearly as important to look for, and value, unrecorded liabilities as it is for unrecorded assets.

CHAPTER TWELVE

Business Combinations

Goal setting has traditionally been based on past performance. This practice has tended to perpetuate the sins of the past.

—*Joseph M. Juran (1904–2008), American economist*

N OW WE COME TO BUSINESS COMBINATIONS—the accountant's term for mergers and acquisitions. Such transactions are normally among the largest a firm ever undertakes, and often some of the most risky. In the long history of business, there never before had been as many large acquisitions as took place in the first decade of the 2000s. This period was the latest of the six historic merger manias that the United States, and to a lesser extent the rest of the financially developed world, has undergone in the past 120 years. The first led to the trusts of the gilded nineties (1893–1904); the second the pyramiding of the roaring twenties (1919–1929); the third the conglomerates of the swinging sixties (1955–1969); the fourth the leveraged buyouts of the junk bond eighties (1974–1989); the fifth the excesses of the dot-com nineties (1993–2000); and finally the real estate naughts (2003–2007). In 2007, at the peak of the latest era, a record $4.5 trillion in cash and securities was spent worldwide on such transactions. Yet in the end the story has nearly always been the same. The initial champagne giddiness gives way to some sort of hangover once the final costs of the deals are tallied.

 ## DO MERGERS PAY OFF?

Michael Porter of Harvard University observed in 1987 that between 50% and 60% of all acquisitions were failures, and some even destroyed shareholder value. Several other studies support this conclusion. Mercer Management Consulting noted that between 1984 and 1994, 60% of the firms in the *BusinessWeek* 500 that had made a major acquisition were less profitable than their industry average. In 2004, McKinsey & Company calculated that only 23% of acquisitions had a positive return on investment. Boston Consulting Group suggested in 2007 that acquisitions transfer value from the acquirer's shareholders to those of the target.

Results vary depending on the type of acquisition, the similarity of the two protagonists, the industry involved, international or domestic competition, and so forth, but the overall trend remains the same: a negative marginal return on investment. None of many attempts—measuring the stock market reaction, valuing the entity after acquisition, determining abnormal returns, or assessing synergies and economies of scale—has been able to isolate the individual impact of an acquisition from the multitude of events that occur all the time in business. There are many explanations for this phenomenon; lack of cultural integration of two different, often competitive entities and failure to achieve promised economies of scale and synergies are the most common.

Revenue Growth Is Essential

Continued profitability is a function of revenue growth. McKinsey & Company, the international strategy consulting firm, demonstrated this in a study of a computer company that had made numerous acquisitions between 2004 and 2009. Assuming all the entities involved had achieved the industry average compound annual growth rate (CAGR) of 6.9%, revenues in 2009 would have been $7,371 million, as shown in Table 12.1, rather than the actual $6,102 million, a 17% shortfall.

Uniform Results

Similar results were found across various fields, regardless of industry, size, or even acquisition experience. Ultimately, revenue growth rather than cost reduction determines the outcome of a merger, and fluctuations can quickly

TABLE 12.1 Expected Revenues from Acquisitions ($ thousands)

Revenues, Base Year 2003	2,148
Acquired revenue	
2004	368
2005	502
2006	94
2007	88
2008	968
	2,020
Subtotal	4,168
Growth @ 6.9%	3,203
Expected revenues	7,371

offset planned cost savings. A 1% shortfall in revenue growth requires 25% greater cost improvements than anticipated to achieve the same bottom line; an extra 2% to 3% in revenue can offset a 50% failure in synergies.

Cost savings are hardly a certainty. McKinsey indicates that up to 40% of mergers fail to capture the anticipated synergies. Stock markets react badly to profit slippage. Failing to meet an earnings target by less than 5% can result in a 15% or more decline in share prices, as the multiple is reduced to reflect expected lower growth. This may scare managements into making cuts in inappropriate places, taking out not just fat, but muscle and even organs.

 ## WHY MERGE?

In view of those problems with mergers and acquisitions, why do so many eager participants pursue them so vigorously in so many fields? Some reasons quoted by managements include the following.

Differential Efficiency

The predominant indicated purpose is differential efficiency. For example, the management of ABC Corporation is more efficient than that of XYZ, Inc. If, after merging, XYZ is brought up to the efficiency of ABC, the overall returns will improve, unless of course a too-high premium over book value was paid. This type of transaction should result in social as well as shareholder gains. Entities operating similar businesses are most likely to succeed in this situation, as they are able to detect below-average performance and have the expertise to improve it.

Operating Synergies

Horizontal mergers between competitors may result in economies of scale or better utilization of capacity. Complementary capabilities, such as overlapping distribution systems or common suppliers and customers, can lead to improvements in efficiencies beyond those available through internal expansion. Provided it does not infringe antitrust laws, which vary greatly between nations, vertical integration (combining firms at different levels of an industry) may also result in beneficial coordination of operations and hence additional profits.

Financial Engineering

A merger combining two or more similar organizations in different parts of the country may result in a lower cost of capital, making both debt and equity funds cheaper. This would be mainly due to lower risks for a larger firm. If the various cash flows are independent, with one making up for a slack period in its counterpart, the possibility of failure is lowered and the cost of debt may be reduced even further. In late 2011, interest rates in most countries are low; therefore a related benefit is that the return on a cash purchase will normally exceed that of money in the bank, which earns about 1% interest, by at least five percentage points.

Undervaluation

Many mergers are stimulated by a build-or-buy choice for the acquirer. If the target is sufficiently undervalued so that additional capacity, at a cost comparable to building it new, could be immediately obtained, the transaction is undoubtedly advantageous. At various times in the past, Tobin's Q ratio (the total enterprise value of a firm divided by the replacement value of its net assets) has been below 1.00% for many entities. If the Q ratio is 0.80 and the average premium over book value is 35%, the resulting purchase price is only 1.08 times the replacement costs of the net assets (the slight enhancement representing the going-concern element).

Changes in Tobin's Q ratio partially explain why merger activity rises and falls during growth and recession periods. This does not, however, apply to intangible assets, which may have a higher value to an acquirer than to the target. For example, a cotton-spinning mill was the most efficient in the industry because it had developed robots that made three independent attempts to fix broken threads on the fly before shutting down the equipment or calling for human assistance. Although they were successful only 30% of the time, the plant was able to deliver more than its rated capacity based on standard downtime. Privately owned, it was acquired at a high price to earnings ratio (PER) by a public company, which then proceeded to apply the technology to all its plants.

Strategic Objectives

One well-established approach to increasing shareholder value is to undertake a merger to achieve a strategic objective, such as geographical expansion, economies of scale, or taking advantage of managerial capabilities that are not fully utilized. Each of these creates synergies, which, to the extent they could be achieved by market participants, are required to be taken into account in determining fair values.

Management Ego

An active market for corporate control has manifested itself in a variety of industries. Acquirers are driven by many of the previously mentioned reasons, but also, in some cases, by ego trips—a motivation for many conglomerates founded on the philosophy that bigger is better (less risky). These combinations also give senior executives an opportunity to enhance their compensation—at least for a few years. But not all ends well, and greedy executives may indeed come at a high price for many owners.

Practice Makes Perfect

Bain & Company, international management consultants, studied managements' behavior at 724 U.S. companies with revenues of more than $500 million, and compared their activity with the returns to shareholders from the 7,475 acquisitions they had made between 1986 and 2001. The firms were divided into the following groups based on their approaches to acquisitions:

- *Constant:* Made acquisitions irrespective of economic cycles
- *Recession:* Increased activities during recessions
- *Growth:* Acted principally in growth periods
- *Doldrums:* Tended to concentrate purchases in periods between recession and growth

The most significant conclusion was that the more deals an entity undertook, the more value it delivered. Those completing over 20 deals in 15 years on average outperformed firms that made 4 or less by 70%, and nonbuyers by almost 100%. While frequency is important, so is continued activity through economic cycles. Constant buyers were by far the most successful, outperforming the growth group by 130% and the doldrums assembly by 80%; the recession category came in second, exceeding the growth group by 40%.

The best performers started with small deals, formalized their processes, and created feedback systems to ensure they would learn from every mistake. Targets were continually reviewed, and promising entities identified. Line management was involved in due diligence, permanent teams were established, and clear parameters devised for integration. Most importantly, constant buyers excelled at saying no. Some parties to a deal, such as investment bankers, often have powerful incentives for it to be consummated, but successful acquirers set a walk-away price and stick to it. Deal making and business building are distinct and not always compatible disciplines. In the long run, the latter is far more important.

With mergers the risk of giving in to wishful thinking is high. Even if the planning is sound, the price right, and the expected synergies achieved, there is a still the chance that Murphy's Law—"Anything that can go wrong will go wrong"—might manifest itself.

 ## DETERMINATION OF SYNERGIES

In planning a business combination and establishing the price to be offered, an acquirer frequently anticipates considerable synergies and strategic advantages resulting from the addition. However, those benefits often fail to materialize to the extent envisaged and, as pointed out in an analysis of 302 major mergers between July 1995 and August 2000 published in *BusinessWeek* (October 4, 2002), overpaying for expected synergies is a major reason for failure. The key to a beneficial transaction is to "pay for what you are getting, not for what you think you will get," and to make sure that the gains are shared fairly between both sets of shareholders.

Synergies are represented by the net incremental discretionary cash flows directly arising from the transaction. They generate much of the hoped-for higher value that the combined enterprise will have over the sum of those of its predecessors. In addition to increasing discretionary cash flows, benefits arising from a merger may also reduce risks associated with operations of either entity and have a positive impact on creating future opportunities.

The fair value of a reporting or cash-generating unit has to take into account the benefits of the anticipated synergies that could be obtained by market participants. This means that fair value is at some strategic level and may be higher than fair market value; of course, as pointed out in Chapter 4, it also may be significantly lower.

 ## INTRINSIC AND INVESTMENT VALUES

When negotiating a purchase price, the acquirer is likely to accept what it is getting as a floor. That is the fair market value of the target as it stands, sometimes called its intrinsic value. The ceiling is what the acquirer thinks it will get, represented by the investment value, which takes into consideration the acquirer's position, planned changes, anticipated expansions, expected future opportunities, and the changed risk profile. The purchase price normally falls between these two amounts, with the benefits split between both sets of shareholders.

 ## QUANTIFICATION

The definition of fair value, together with its relationship to fair market value, was discussed in Chapter 2. It assumes that the acquirer is able to obtain those synergies available to market participants. If they are not realized and the fair value of the net assets acquired turns out to be less than the amount paid, a goodwill impairment loss will likely occur.

Synergies fall into two broad categories: those that increase revenues and those that lower costs; both may affect the amount paid for the target.

Factors that may increase revenues include:

- Cross-selling of complementary items
- Integration of product lines
- Diversification of customers
- Better use of sales channels and marketing programs
- Higher selling prices

Factors that may save costs:

- Accelerated entry to the target's business
- Improved economies of scale
- Increased purchasing power and volume discounts
- Lower cost of capital
- Access to better technology
- Secure source of supplies
- Elimination of duplicate administrative activities
- Reduced capital expenditures
- Improved use of working capital
- Better capacity utilization and productivity

Integrating an acquirer and a target normally leads to extra expenses, one-time occurrences not often subjected to the same level of analysis as applied to predicted revenue increases and cost reductions. They frequently exceed the budget and sometimes the acquirer's wildest expectations. In applying ASC 805 or IFRS 3, this characteristic must be taken into account. Potential extra costs are listed below; some are one-time expenses, and others will be spread over more than one reporting period:

- Temporary double management
- Severance pay
- Combining sales forces, control, and information systems
- Dealing with overlapping customer relationships
- Transferring personnel
- Monitoring the integration
- Terminating leases
- Additional legal activities
- Unforeseen actions of competitors
- Miscellaneous contingencies
- Assimilating the different business cultures
- Company moving costs

Fair Values

Synergies are difficult to value directly, so they are often quantified by the difference between the investment and intrinsic values of the target (discussed above). Both values are established separately for existing operations, emerging activities, and future opportunities.

The intrinsic value of existing operations is commonly obtained by capitalizing current earnings. Emerging activities are almost always valued by discounting projected cash flows, whereas future opportunities will usually be given little weight until the target's management provides details. In all cases, a method under the market approach should be used as confirmation, if it is not chosen as the primary method.

For investment value, FASB and IASB recommend the discounted cash flow (DCF) method, but do not differentiate among existing operations, emerging activities, and future opportunities. While their suggestion is satisfactory for the first two, the real-option method is often more helpful for future opportunities. It is relatively easy to realistically reflect the expected synergies and extra expenses in DCF values by including management's forecasts rather than market participants' projections for:

- The perceived benefits
- Costs associated with them
- Timing of their realization

The probable risks linked to the realization of the anticipated benefits should be reflected in the discount rate, which will likely be lower for investment value rather than intrinsic value.

When it is difficult to establish the timing of the perceived benefits, or the chances of obtaining them, a satisfactory solution is to estimate the amounts and related costs for various scenarios. They should be prepared separately for the investment values of existing operations, emerging activities, and future opportunities and then weighted by their probabilities. In such circumstances, the elements of the First Chicago method should be applied. This technique, often used for venture capital investments, projects the operations of a business for three to five years into the future using three scenarios (success, survival, and failure). It then calculates the weighted present value of the potential exit prices. When applied to synergies the scenarios are:

- *Success.* The expected conservative postacquisition synergies are realized.
- *Survival.* Half of the expected synergies are achieved.
- *Failure.* No synergies are realized.

As the risks associated with the realization of the benefits are reflected in the probabilities, all three scenarios would use the same discount rate.

Strategic Advantages

Certain benefits from an acquisition may not have an identifiable impact on the cash flows and therefore are generally strategic advantages rather than synergies. Treating them as reductions in specific risks is preferable (see Chapter 8) when using a buildup method to establish the discount rate; examples are:

- ▪ Diminished competition
- ▪ Increased market share
- ▪ Incremental growth opportunities
- ▪ Lower financial volatility

Timing of Realization

One of the most common errors in planning an acquisition is underestimating the time it will take to realize the expected synergies. This is often related to the difficulty of integrating the target's culture with that of the acquirer. It is virtually impossible to increase revenue, if, for example, the marketing and distribution arms of the two firms cannot coordinate their efforts because one is highly centralized and the other geographically diversified.

Noncore Activities

In nearly every acquisition, the target is carrying on some activities that have a limited fit with the major functions of the combined enterprise. In the past, many businesses attempted to reduce risks and accelerate growth by diversifying into product and service areas not directly related to their core business. Now such elements are usually sold.

Conglomerate Discount

When the value of an enterprise is less than that of the total of its component entities, the firm is described as suffering from a conglomerate discount. An example was Seagram, the successful distiller, which in 1981 obtained effective control of DuPont through a 24% holding. That firm's profits represented 70% of reported earnings, but, as only dividends were recorded in cash flows, the company PER declined, ostensibly due to "lack of focus." Later (1995), in an attempt to generate growth, management sold the DuPont holding back to that company for $9 billion cash, much of which was spent on all the shares of Universal Studios, the film and music empire. After Seagram's acquisition by Vivendi, the original liquor business was sold off in bits and pieces. The net result was a decline of over 50% in the controlling family's fortune.

In assessing the synergies of an acquisition, it is essential to determine which operations or assets are noncore and to decide early when and at what price they could be sold. The fundamental methodology is to separate the target into its components and value each separately. While comparable transactions can provide some benchmarks, remember that no two companies are alike in regard to risks or potential cash flows. Careful analyses will ensure that the comparable transactions are truly comparable.

A major reason for a conglomerate discount is a lack of information at the reporting or cash-generating unit level. This creates risks, which always result in lower values, no matter what the source. Items that are difficult to determine for the acquirer are the transaction and tax costs associated with breaking up parts of the entity. After the merger is completed, finding buyers for the so-called orphans may take longer and be more costly than anticipated, because when their availability becomes known, bargain hunters will appear. The acquirer must also consider the possibility of being left with unwanted units for which no buyers can be found at a reasonable price. In such cases, there can only be speculation about the eventual form of divestiture (e.g., asset or share sale, spin-off, etc.).

Genuine Assets

In an article in *Strategic Finance* magazine (November 2000), Joel Litman of Diamond Technology Partners, a Chicago strategy consulting firm, pointed out that most entities have genuine assets that are not shown on any financial statement, except perhaps as part of goodwill, because they do not qualify for accounting purposes as intangible assets. Some examples are:

Relationships
- Unique partners and alliances
- Key vendors
- Unique competitor relationships
- Unique government relationships
- Financier links
- Special employee/union relationships

Attention
- "Eyeballs"
- Traffic: foot, vehicle, other
- Mental attention

Technology
- Hardware infrastructure

Brand Equity
- Reputation
- Awareness

Intellectual Capital
- In-house technical expertise
- Specialized market experience
- Research and development
- Unique data or information

Processes
- Core competencies
- Economies of scale or scope

Financing
- Access to equity
- Access to cheap debt

Management
- Special characteristics of the board and management, such as industry relationships
- Reputation
- Leadership
- Teamwork
- Deep bench

Workforce
- Access to personnel for peak and trough
- Work flow management
- Good employee culture
- Employee knowledge
- Strong recruiting capabilities

Management should be questioned about such items and their values should be reconciled with the residual amount recorded as goodwill.

CHAPTER THIRTEEN

Purchase Price Allocation

Successful investing is anticipating the anticipation of others.

—*John Maynard (Lord) Keynes (1883–1946),*

British economist

AFTER A BUSINESS COMBINATION IS CLOSED, the real valuation work begins. Both the Financial Accounting Standards Board (FASB) and the International Accounting Standards Board (IASB) require that an acquirer be identified and that all the assets and technologies acquired and the liabilities and contingencies assumed of the target (the acquired entity) be recorded for consolidation purposes, at their fair values. The difference between the total fair value of the net assets acquired and that of the consideration is ascribed to goodwill. This process is described as a purchase price allocation (PPA).

Preparing a PPA report can be a daunting task unless one is already familiar with all parts of the process—not only the governing rules and standards but also the sometimes complex valuation methods involved, especially for intangible assets. It is tempting to leave everything to the valuators and auditors; unfortunately, management is responsible. The valuators are only advisors;

they deliver the facts (sometimes as ranges) but do not make the final decisions. Nor do the auditors, who only verify the reasonableness of the conclusions and supporting data. Frequently, managers are surprised by last-minute questions or astonished by the impact on profits of the amortization of the (new) fair values of both assets and liabilities. This chapter is intended to give preparers and users an understanding of the procedures to help avoid unnecessary hassles.

The PPA process has five interconnected stages:

1. Determine the acquirer.
2. Establish the consideration's fair value.
3. Identify all the items involved.
4. Select appropriate valuation techniques.
5. Estimate fair values and reconcile rates of return.

This chapter does not include a review of ASC 805, *Business Combinations*, or IFRS 3, *Business Combinations*, nor discussions of the appropriate valuation methods; most of the latter are found in other chapters. It merely deals with the process, together with the structure and contents of the accompanying report.

STAGE 1: DETERMINE THE ACQUIRER

Determining the acquirer is not always obvious, or indeed as easy as one might think; the two parties, the acquirer and the target, are identified by applying the concept of control. This is the power to govern the financial and operating policies of an entity to obtain benefits from its activities. Although the FASB and IASB have not defined them, operating policies generally relate to sales, marketing, manufacturing, human resources, and investment functions, while financial policies cover budgeting, credit terms, securities issuance, cash management, capital expenditures, and accounting practices.

Control

Control encompasses the notions of both governance and its economic consequences—benefits and risks. When an entity has the power to govern another's policies but derives no benefits from its activities, there is a presumption that control does not exist; an example is a limited partnership where a general partner may be responsible for management for a fee but have no other participation. When one entity (the parent) owns, directly or indirectly, more than half of the voting power of another, control is presumed; however, in exceptional circumstances, it may be possible to demonstrate that such ownership does not constitute control. When the parent owns half or less of the voting power but has the power, by whatever means, to appoint or remove the majority of the governing body or to cast the majority of votes at meetings of the group, control also exists. When two entities have joint control (i.e., together they are able to exercise power), it is likely effectively a joint venture, subject to ASC 323, *Investments—Equity Method and Joint Ventures*, or IFRS 11, *Joint Arrangements*.

Potential Voting Rights

An entity may own instruments (e.g., share purchase warrants or options, or debt or equity instruments convertible into voting shares) that have the potential, if exercised or converted, to give the entity additional voting power or reduce another party's voting power. Such potential voting rights are not considered under U.S. Generally Accepted Accounting Principles (GAAP), but, if they are immediately exercisable, are important in determining the acquirer for International Financial Reporting Standards (IFRS). In either case, the proportions of profit or loss and changes in equity allocated to the parent and noncontrolling interests are determined by existing ownership and not by any voting rights. In assessing whether potential voting rights contribute to control, all the facts and circumstances that affect them should be considered, including exercise terms and other contractual arrangements; however, management's intentions and financial ability to exercise or convert such rights are irrelevant.

Where the concept of context does not clearly indicate which entity is the acquirer, other factors have to be considered, as shown in Table 13.1.

TABLE 13.1 Other Factors Affecting Control

Factor	Acquirer Is
Consideration primarily cash, other assets, or incurred liabilities	Usually the entity that transfers the cash or other assets or incurs the liabilities
Consideration primarily equity	Usually the entity that issues its equity; however, in a reverse merger, the target may issue equity
Relative size	Usually the entity whose relative size (assets, revenues, or profit) is significantly greater
More than two combining entities	Usually the one that initiated the combination; however, also consider relative sizes
New entity that issues equity	The combining entity whose owners receive the largest portion of the equity that existed before the combination, identified by applying the guidance in other paragraphs
New entity that transfers cash or other assets or incurs liabilities	New entity

STAGE 2: ESTABLISH THE CONSIDERATION'S FAIR VALUE

Determining the consideration's fair value is also not always as easy as it might appear; however, it is very important as it directly affects the amount of goodwill recorded or, in a few cases, the nature of a bargain purchase. The consideration may include cash; selected financial, physical, or intangible assets; another business; debt securities; shares of various types; and other financial instruments—for example, share purchase warrants—as well as contingent consideration such as earnouts or contingent value rights. Some payments to former owners may not be in exchange for the business: examples are for services, use of property, or profit sharing. Those amounts are treated separately and expensed as appropriate. When anything other than cash is part of the consideration, the acquirer measures it at fair value as of the transaction date, which is when control of the target is obtained, using techniques discussed in previous chapters.

Example

To demonstrate the process, we consider the purchase of California Technologies Inc., a component manufacturer, on December 31, 2007, a normal period, before the 2008 Great Recession when many markets became inactive. The price was $110,000,000, paid as follows:

	Nominal Amount ($000)	Fair Value ($000)
Cash	40,000	40,000
Non–interest-bearing notes due equally in 1, 2 and 3 years	30,000	28,055
Shares of foreign parent	30,000	23,775
Earnout—based on increase in EBITDA	10,000	3,893
	110,000	95,723

Other than cash, each nominal amount required adjusting to be recorded at fair value.

Non–Interest-Bearing Notes

The notes were issued by a domestic acquisition subsidiary in U.S. funds and guaranteed by the parent, an Asian multinational. In the Eurodollar market, it borrowed at the London Inter-Bank Offered Rate (LIBOR), which at the time was about 50 basis points (bp; 100 bp = 1 percentage point) over U.S. Treasuries. This gave rates for the one-year note of 2.97%; two-year note, 3.33%; and three-year note, 3.66%. The fair values of the notes were therefore the face amounts discounted for their terms at such rates.

	Nominal Amount ($000)	Fair Value ($000)
One-year note	10,000	9,711
Two-year note	10,000	9,366
Three-year note	10,000	8,978
	30,000	28,055

Shares of Foreign Parent

The shares of the foreign parent were listed on a local stock exchange, but according to national law, there was a one-year holding period for private placements, which the transaction was considered to be. The discount for this was obtained by using the Black-Scholes model assuming put-call parity to calculate the cost of a 12-month put; with an expected volatility of 56%, the discount was 20.75%, reducing the $30 million nominal amount to a fair value of $23,775,000.

Earnout

The earnout was 2.0 times the increase in the 2008 earnings before interest, taxes, depreciation, and amortization (EBITDA) over those for 2007, to a maximum of $10 million, payable at the end of 2008. Management believed the most likely (75% probability) increase in the EBITDA would be $2,675,000. The fair value of the earnout was therefore $3,893,000, being $2,675,000 × 2 × 75% ($4,012,500) discounted for one year.

Consideration

The total fair value of the consideration was $95,723,000, an overall discount from the nominal amount of 13%, a not-inconsequential figure.

Replacement Option Awards

Often acquirers will issue share options to employees of the target to replace existing awards that were tied, at least in part, to the target's shares. Those are intended to ensure that the target's employees are in a similar economic position immediately after, as they were before, the business combination. The replacement awards may also include additional service requirements, encouraging employees to remain after the transaction. Such awards are consideration if they relate to past services or compensation if they cover future activities.

Replacement awards are considered modifications in accordance with ASC 718, *Stock Based Compensation*, or IFRS 2, *Share-Based Payment*. The acquirer must analyze the situation to determine whether it is obligated to replace the target's awards. This will be so if the target or its employees have the ability to enforce replacement or if it is required by (1) an agreement, (2) the terms of the target's awards, or (3) applicable laws or regulations. If it is an obligation, then a portion of the fair value of the replacement awards is consideration, the remainder compensation. ASC 805 provides guidance on calculating the attributable portions.

 ## KNOWLEDGE OF THE INDUSTRY

Before undertaking the remaining three steps of the purchase price allocation process, a valuator should research the target. A proper PPA report will demonstrate a thorough understanding of: the acquired business; the industry in which it operates; all of its assets, liabilities, revenues, and expenses; and its historical financial performance; as well as the purpose and structure of the transaction. Inquiries, analytical procedures, and adjustments to the reported financial statements are essential in order to reach reasonable conclusions as to the various fair values involved.

The investigations must include: the target's operating characteristics, production methods, types of products and services, distribution systems, operating locations, compensation methods, material transactions with related parties, and a tour of at least one plant. Much information will come from discussions with management and staff, reading pertinent publications, searches on the Internet, and other due diligence, all of which contribute to a comprehensive view of the industry and the firm. The objective is to establish those characteristics of the target and the competitive environment that play a material role in its fair value.

Analytical Procedures

Before the valuator meets with the target's management, he or she should analyze that firm's financial statements to identify areas requiring additional information. This work provides a basis for questions about relationships between items or items that appear unusual. In addition, the target's accounting policies and practices should be carefully examined to determine how they differ from those of the acquirer. Typical analytical procedures consist of:

- Comparing the latest financial statements with those for previous periods (e.g., quarterly, annual), using trend and ratio analyses
- Identifying plausible relationships based on knowledge of the entity and its industry
- Using such relationships to confirm that management's expectations are reasonable
- Checking actual results against available budgets, forecasts, projections, and business plans
- Studying interrelationships, such as variations in sales against related costs or changes in additions to property, plant & equipment (PP&E), compared with changes for depreciation, amortization, maintenance, and repairs

Inquiries

When reviewing and adjusting an audited target's financial statements, management's responses to the following questions are important:

- Are they in conformity with GAAP or IFRS? Were the standards consistently applied?
- What effect did the differences from the acquirer's accounting policies and practices have on past profits and the current balance sheet?
- Who is to adjust the financial statements used for the PPA process to reflect the acquirer's accounting treatments?
- What unusual or complex situations in the past two fiscal years had a bearing on the historical financial statements? Are further adjustments necessary?
- Did any significant transactions in the last reporting period affect either entity's outlook?
- Have all adjustments from any previous audit or review engagements been recorded?
- Since the announcement of the transaction, have any events occurred that could have a bearing on the financial statements that will be used for the PPA?

- What significant accruals, capitalizations, or other adjustments will influence future reported income?
- Is management aware of any investigation into suspected fraud affecting the target?
- Has any regulatory agency informed the target of any possible investigation?
- What actions of the target's board of directors or shareholders have affected the financial statements?
- Are any reports available from previous audits or reviews of significant components of the target, its subsidiaries, or other investees?
- Have all acquired intangible assets been identified?
- Have any material weaknesses under Sarbanes-Oxley Act Section 404, or an equivalent statute, been identified?

There is no need to corroborate management's answers with additional evidence, but valuators should always weigh their reasonableness and consistency in light of other procedures, their general experience, and industry knowledge.

STAGE 3: IDENTIFY ALL THE ITEMS INVOLVED

After completing an acquisition, many companies do not know exactly what they have bought, as the price is normally based on some mix of historical earnings, projected future cash flows, and the expected benefits of synergies. In every case, a rigorous analysis of what the acquirer has actually received is essential. This will almost certainly involve unrecognized assets, as well as hidden liabilities. The discussions in the PPA report on the various assets acquired should identify them and detail the characteristics that are significant to the valuation. It will also include an overview of any relevant technical guidance and acceptable techniques regarding each particular class—financial, physical, and intangible.

Financial Assets

The initial step of Stage 3 is fairly simple; it is to identify the tangible assets, normally found on the balance sheet, and determine their fair values. Even items such as tools, molds, jigs, and dies that have been completely written off will have been recorded in past financial statements. At this point, everything else is classified as an intangible. The best starting point is the financial assets, which are usually the easiest to value. For many there are markets offering Level 1 or Level 2 inputs. Others that are material to the target, especially receivables, will need adjustments, as their fair values are the amounts expected to be received discounted to the transaction date.

Physical Assets

Physical assets cover three categories of inventories and another eight or more for PP&E. Inventory is initially recognized at the lower of cost or market, which is generally the price paid for it. In a business combination, the fair value of the target's inventories is presumed to be its cost to the acquirer. This does not result in an immediate write-down after the transaction, even though they typically exceed replacement costs because part of the target's manufacturing profit is included.

Inventories—Materials and Supplies

The fair values of materials and supplies inventories represent the prices a market participant would receive to sell them in a current transaction in the principal market (or in its absence, the most advantageous market), not the target's cost. The choice of market is considered from the perspective of the acquirer, which may result in differences among entities. As location is often an attribute of inventories, the indicated price is adjusted for the costs to transport them to or from the market.

If an acquirer purchased inventories from the target before the business combination, consideration must be given to their carrying value. When the purchase was in an arm's-length transaction, the acquirer should not eliminate the profit recorded by the target on these items.

Inventories—Work in Process

The fair value of acquired work in process is calculated in a manner similar to that for finished goods; normally it is based on a market participant's estimated selling price for the final product, adjusted for the costs of (1) completion of the manufacturing process, (2) the necessary marketing effort, and (3) an appropriate profit. The costs to complete should include all relevant expenses, as shown in Table 13.2.

TABLE 13.2 Expenses That May Be Relevant to Investors

Expense	Relevant	Excluded
Equipment production repairs and maintenance	X	
Utilities of production area	X	
Rents of production area	X	
Indirect labor and production supervision, including all benefits	X	
Indirect materials and supplies	X	
Tools and equipment not capitalized	X	
Quality control and inspection	X	
Distribution and warehousing	X	
Transportation of goods for resale from a warehouse to retail stores	X	
Unreimbursed shipments to customers		X
General and administrative expenses		X
Executive salaries		X
Depreciation on production assets	X	
Plant administration	X	
Rework labor, scrap, and spoilage		X
Insurance repurchasing, production, and warehousing	X	
Marketing, advertising, and selling		X
Research and development		X
Royalties		X
Theft		X
Purchasing materials and supplies	X	
Data processing for purchasing, warehousing, and shipping	X	
Income taxes		X
Interest	Some assets	Normally
Package design		X

Inventories—Finished Goods

In a business combination, finished goods inventories are usually measured at selling price less costs to sell. Level 2 inputs include either a retail price to customers or a wholesale price to retailers, adjusted for differences between the condition and location of the inventories and the comparable market items. Fair values are intended to reflect the amounts that would be received in a transaction to sell the inventory to a market participant that would finish the sales process. Conceptually, fair value should be the same, whether adjustments are made to a retail price (downward) or to a wholesale price (upward). Generally, the one that requires the least amount of subjective changes should be used.

In most cases, the fair value of acquired finished goods inventory is determined by using a market participant's estimated selling price, either retail or wholesale depending on the circumstances, adjusted for both the selling expenses and a normal profit for the effort. Selling expenses are the incremental costs directly related to the inventory based on assumptions expected from market participants. The costs are those that would not have been incurred had the inventory not been produced, such as transportation, packaging, direct marketing, and sales commissions; overhead not attributable to the inventory is excluded, while directly related costs are acceptable. The normal profit for the effort should be less than the margin expected by the acquirer for items produced after the transaction, because the results of selling efforts by the target are part of the fair value.

Property, Plant & Equipment

Property (land, buildings, and leasehold improvements), plant (machinery, piping, or other apparatus attached to a structure) & equipment (items that can be easily removed, such as vehicles, furniture, and electronics) acquired in a business combination are measured at fair values. Their estimated remaining useful lives (RULs) are based on the expected uses by the acquirer; the target's RULs are not carried over.

Much PP&E is subject to legal obligations associated with its retirement, such as the removal of asbestos from a factory before its demolition. The asset retirement obligations (AROs) are recognized at fair value as of the acquisition date, as a separate liability (see Chapter 11). PP&E to be sold is classified as such and carried at fair value less costs to sell.

Leasehold improvements, like other PP&E, are measured at fair value as of the acquisition date, and their RULs reevaluated. This is true despite ASC 805 prohibiting an acquirer from changing the target's classification of a lease unless it is modified as part of the transaction. Such improvements are amortized over the shorter of either the RUL or a term that includes the existing lease period and renewals that are deemed to be reasonably assured. This is determined based on whether any renewal rights are bargain options, or if failure to renew would impose a significant penalty. When the target has significant leasehold improvements, the acquirer may assume that the renewals are reasonably assured, as the loss on the improvements from a failure to renew would be significant; those renewal rights determine the RUL of the improvements.

Mineral rights consist of the legal right to explore, extract, and retain at least a portion of the benefits from mineral deposits. Mining assets, including mineral rights, are considered physical assets and classified as a separate component of PP&E in the notes to the financial statements. In estimating the fair value of mineral assets, an acquirer should take into account both the value beyond proven and probable reserves to the extent that a market participant would include it in determining the fair value of the asset, as well as the effects of anticipated fluctuations in the future market prices of minerals in a manner that is consistent with the expectations of marketplace participants.

Independent real estate and technical appraisers are typically required to determine the fair values of all PP&E; in doing so, they apply the highest and best use concept discussed in Chapter 3. For property, this is not necessarily the existing application, while for plant and equipment, it will normally be their present function. It is essential to include all items, such as molds, tools, jigs, and dies, that may be fully written off but are still in use.

Intangible Assets

After dealing with the financial and physical (tangible) items (both assets and liabilities), the focus shifts to the most difficult arena—intangible assets. To be recorded, they have to meet the FASB and IASB's test of being either contractual/legal or separable. They are normally divided into:

- *Marketing related:* Trademarks, Internet domain names, noncompete agreements, and so on
- *Customer related:* Customer lists, contracts and relationships, order backlogs, and so forth
- *Contract based:* Royalty agreements, service/supply contracts, leases, franchises, and the like
- *Technology based:* Technology, software, databases, trade secrets, and so on
- *Artistic related:* Literary works, musical works, pictures, videos, and so forth
- *Government granted:* Licenses for TV stations, cellular phone systems, taxicabs, and so on

Although it meets a criterion, an assembled workforce or human capital is deemed part of goodwill, but its fair value has to be calculated as that amount is needed in applying several of the accepted valuation methodologies for other items. The goal is to establish each identifiable intangible asset involved, and then determine its fair value. Any residual amount is goodwill. In every case, the three traditional approaches—cost, market, and income—are considered.

When an item is categorized as an intangible asset, three questions arise: What is its value in use? Is the economic transfer price different? What is its remaining useful life? Every intangible asset may be considered as a bundle of rights that can be transferred either for a limited period or completely. Separate legal and economic interests derived from them give rise to the cash flows that form the bases of their values in use. The following list covers most allotments of rights from economic and valuation perspectives. If there is doubt as to which rights have been transferred and which retained, the assistance of legal counsel should be obtained.

- Licensees or franchisees are granted specific rights generally restricted by geography, type, term, and application. The use of the name "McDonald's," the golden arches symbol, and that company's hamburger production system are granted by contract. Sublicensees or subfranchisees receive certain rights transferred to them by a franchisee or licensee.
- Owners, franchisors, or licensors normally retain residual rights while selling or transferring others. Those retained rights relate to ownership privileges and a flow of royalties from the franchisees or licensees.
- Life interests restrict the rights owned or transferred to another party to the lifetime of either the owner or the recipient. A life estate entitles an individual to the income from the rights only during his or her lifetime. Term interests restrict to a specific period the rights owned or transferred, and their existence is terminated after that time.
- Terminal or reversionary rights are returned to the original owner on the expiration of a certain period or the completion of the specific task for which they have been transferred.
- Fractional ownership rights relate to a partial interest in the bundle of rights that make up the intangible asset.

Intellectual Property

Certain intangible assets known as intellectual property are legally protected. Three of them—trademarks, copyrights, and trade secrets—are discussed in the following subsections; patents are omitted as they are well known.

Trademarks

Trademarks are words, names, symbols, or other devices used to indicate the source of the product and distinguish it from others. A service mark identifies the originator of a service rather than a product. Collective marks are used to identify goods or services of members of a group. Certification marks verify the geographic origin or other characteristics of a good or service. Trademarks, service, collective, and certification marks may be protected legally through registration with national trademark offices or, in some countries, by continuous commercial use. Unlike patents and copyrights, trademarks sometimes do not have a fixed legal life span. An enterprise may recognize, as a single asset apart from goodwill, a group of complementary intangible assets commonly referred to as a brand when the items comprising it have similar useful lives.

Copyrights

A copyright is a bundle of exclusive rights that provides authors of literary, musical, dramatic, and artistic works, as well as computer software, with the sole right to authorize the following uses of their works: to produce all or part of the work; to make new versions; to distribute copies by selling, renting, leasing, or lending them; to perform (e.g., recite, play, dance, or act) the work publicly; or to display the work publicly, directly, or by means of film, television, slides, or other devices or processes. The first three rights are violated when anyone copies, excerpts, adapts, or publishes a copyrighted work without permission. Unless the facts prove otherwise, it should be assumed that all published original works are protected by copyright.

Ownership of a copyright may become an issue when the creator is engaged by an organization, either individually or as part of a group. As the copyright will belong to the entity, there are few problems when the person is an employee. For example, if a firm hires an individual to develop software, the firm usually owns legal title to the resulting asset. However, if the employee, either alone or as part of a group, is under contract, he or she may choose to only grant a license and use the retained ownership to generate income. Thus, when valuing an intangible asset, it would be foolish to assume who is the actual owner without carefully determining all factors associated with it.

Under the U.S. Copyright Extension Act, an individual's copyright lasts 75 years after his or her death, while for-hire copyrights (generated by employees) owned by firms expire 95 years after publication. Although legally considered artistic-related for copyright purposes, engineering designs and drawings are intellectual property under the Uniform Trade Secrets Act (see the technology-based section later in this chapter).

Valuation Methods for Copyrights

As copyrights grant legal monopolies for considerable periods, they are usually valued under the income approach by one of the following methods:

- *Profit split analysis.* The total estimated income that can be generated from a given copyright is split among all the enterprise activities that earn it.
- *Royalty income analysis.* This is an estimate of the royalty income the copyright could generate if licensed to others.
- *Incremental analysis.* This is the estimated difference between the incomes generated using the copyright and what the entity would earn without owning it.

Trade Secrets

A trade secret is information, including a formula, pattern, compilation, program, device, method, technique, or process that derives independent economic value or potential from not being generally known, and is the subject of efforts that are reasonable under the circumstances to maintain its secrecy. Trade secrets are not registered by governments but are maintained through their owner's precautions. In the United States, the Uniform Trade Secrets Act, variations of which have been adopted in 36 states, generally standardizes the law by defining trade secrets and the protection accorded them. Matters of public or general knowledge within an industry cannot be trade secrets.

Elements to be considered in determining what information might be a trade secret include: the extent to which it is known outside the business, the number of employees aware of it, how it is protected, how it is of value to the business and its competitors, and whether it could be duplicated with ease. In essence, the protection of trade secrets by law is available only if the owner has taken appropriate steps to maintain and assure confidentiality and proprietary ownership. Trade secret and copyright laws protect the same kinds of information, but are sometimes mutually exclusive. However, they have some economic and legal similarities, and under the Copyright Extension Act they can work together. Both are available for unpublished works as long as the idea (or ideas) is sufficiently innovative to qualify as a trade secret and the information is kept confidential. They both may be available for works that are distributed on a limited and restricted basis under arrangements requiring the licensee (user) to recognize and maintain the trade secret aspects of the work.

This dual protection is especially pertinent for computer software, as trade secret protection is generally not available if the source code is made available to the public on an unrestricted basis. Works that are widely distributed without specific licensing agreements will generally lose their trade secret status, but may still be entitled to copyright protection. The deposit of a physical copy with the U.S. Copyright Office of the work that is being registered effectively discloses any trade secrets involved. There are several methods for simultaneously registering a computer program and maintaining secrets; the most common is to withhold the source code altogether and only deposit the object code, which is impossible to understand when read, in the U.S. Copyright Office.

STAGE 4: SELECT APPROPRIATE VALUATION TECHNIQUES

This section discusses how certain assets found in nearly all entities are normally valued, again using as an example California Technologies Inc., whose purchase consideration was discussed in Stage 2. The items involved are customer relationships, trade names, technologies, assembled workforce, and PP&E.

Customer Relationships

Customer relationships are usually valued under the income approach using a discounted cash flows method. Key assumptions are required for: attrition rate—how fast existing customers are anticipated to leave; expected (EBIT or EBITDA) margins; and contributory asset charges—the notional costs for use of other essential items (financial, tangible, and intangible assets plus the assembled workforce).

The target's industry functioned as if the European and American markets differed. In reality, both were supplied mainly from Asia. From 2004 to 2007, the unit price in euros (unconverted) differed by less than 5% from the similar dollar cost in the United States. In April 2004, European sales were €46.40 ($56.50) a unit, compared with $43.00 in the United States; three years later the euro price was €47.10 ($73.30) against $47.10 in the United States. As a result, in 2007, European gross margins were about 26.3% compared with 10.2% for the United States. Management expected this benefit to continue, as the target had strong links with German buyers; therefore, the value of the customer relationships was based on the price premium disappearing over 10 years. The amount ascribed was $6.7 million, the present value at 25% of the net benefits for the next 10 years from projected sales to European customers; it reflected contributory charges for capital expenditures, working capital, assembled workforce, and trade name.

Trade Names and Technologies

Trade names, technologies, and other similar intangible assets are typically valued using the relief-from-royalty method; this was discussed with an example in Chapter 3 and Chapter 6. It is based on the concept that the fair value of such an item is the present value of what an entity is willing to pay for its use, if it is not owned. Our manufacturer's trade name was ascribed a market-based royalty of 2.75%, giving a fair value of $11.6 million, the present value at 25% of the after-tax savings from ownership using 10 years' projected sales with 3% subsequent growth. A similar calculation gave $15.5 million for the technology.

Assembled Workforce

An example of calculating fair value of an assembled workforce is found in Chapter 7; in this case, it was $3,250,000 which is treated as part of goodwill.

Property, Plant & Equipment

Independent real estate and technical appraisers are recommended to determine fair values for PP&E, as they have many peculiarities. It is important to include all fully written-off but still useful items, such as molds, tools, jigs, and dies, which are normally valued by the cost approach. Necessary molds, with an indefinite physical life, had been written off; their fair value is their adjusted replacement cost of $1,325,000.

The manufacturer's assets included a great deal of unrecorded know-how (trade secrets) relating to its major plant (specialized furnaces). When bought in 2000, the firm obtained 48 mothballed (nonfunctioning) examples at $50,000 each. At the valuation date (2007), half were in service with a replacement cost of $600,000 each; but the know-how allows each remaining unit to be rehabilitated for only $150,000. Engineering studies indicate they have an economic/physical life of 25 years, substantially similar to the 30 years specified for new units.

The fair value of the 24 operating units was $11.4 million ($475,000 each, considering the four factors). The present value of future savings in rebuilding the others is $4,671,000 over three years, in addition to their $1.2 million book value, giving a total of $17,271,000 for the furnaces.

STAGE 5: ESTIMATE FAIR VALUES AND RECONCILE RATES OF RETURN

Table 13.3 analyzes what was really received by the new owner of California Technologies. It actually paid $95,723,000 for a business with normalized pre-tax profits of $9,328,000, equivalent to $5,970,000 of net income. The effective capitalization rate was 6.2% (PER of 16.0 times) compared with a nominal PER of 18.4 times (5.4%) on the reported purchase price of $110 million.

For amortization, the trade name is considered an intangible asset with an indefinite life, while the technologies and supply contracts each have an RUL of five years. No tax benefit has been included, as the structure of the deal resulted in a U.S. tax rate of only 15% and no foreign tax payments are anticipated.

The book value and fair value of each asset, together with the expected weighted average return on assets (WARA), are set out in Table 13.3. The goodwill of $15,093,000, including the workforce, represents 15.8% of the total net assets received—about a normal level.

TABLE 13.3 California Technologies PPA Reconciliation ($ thousands)

	Cost	Accumulated Depreciation	Net Book Value	Fair Value	WARA Rate	Indicated Return
Consideration				95,723	9.6%	9,189
Tangible Assets Acquired						
Current						
Cash			3,421	3,421	1.5%	51
Receivables			1,995	1,895	3.5%	66
Inventories			7,267	7,930	6.0%	476
Prepaids			4,198	4,198	0.0%	—
			16,881	17,444	3.4%	593

(continued)

TABLE 13.3 *(Continued)*

	Cost	Accumulated Depreciation	Net Book Value	Fair Value	WARA Rate	Indicated Return
Capital						
Land	1,204		1,204	1,300	4.5%	59
Building	2,312	(215)	2,097	2,600	5.5%	143
Furnaces	904	(429)	475	17,271	7.0%	1,209
Machinery and equipment	5,292	(1,247)	4,045	3,925	8.0%	314
Molds, jigs, tools, and dies	1,567	(1,567)	—	1,325	8.5%	113
			7,821	26,421	7.0%	1,837
Deposits						
Material			22,825	22,825	8.0%	1,826
Utilities			254	254	0.0%	—
			23,079	23,079	7.9%	1,826
Total			47,781	66,944	6.4%	4,257
Liabilities Assumed						
Payables and accruals			(2,481)	(2,481)	0.0%	—
Leases			(4,150)	(4,150)	6.8%	(282)
Term loan			(11,583)	(11,583)	5.2%	(602)
			(18,214)	(18,214)	4.9%	(885)
Book Equity Purchased			29,567	48,730	6.9%	3,372
Unrecorded Assets Obtained						
Trade name				11,600	12.0%	1,392
Technologies				15,500	12.0%	1,860
Supply contracts				4,800	10.0%	480
Assembled workforce				3,250	11.0%	358
Goodwill				11,843	15.8%	1,867
				46,993	12.7%	5,957
Net Assets Received				95,723	9.7%	9,329

CONCLUSION

Preparing a PPA report is a complex technical process. In many ways it is more difficult than valuing an overall business, as in it management and valuators must assess numerous cash flows and establish rates of return applicable to each of them. Although every transaction presents different circumstances, there are a few general rules.

The report should be well supported so that a reader is able to follow the process step-by-step. It must demonstrate knowledge of all relevant facts and circumstances pertaining to the transaction so the reader may rely on the conclusions. Supporting documents must be clearly listed and the narrative sufficiently detailed, so that the methods used for the various items can be easily understood. A report will not make sense if it describes unsound processes or even reasonable valuation processes in abbreviated, ambiguous, or dense language. Clearly written, it should reflect the economic reality of the acquisition within the fair value accounting rules.

CHAPTER FOURTEEN

Impairment

In the ideal system, there's a let's-pretend auctioneer who runs around and collects all the chits of the buyers and the sellers. If they *don't* match up, the auctioneer keeps running around until the market clears. Now buyers and sellers are effectively boycotting the pretend auctioneer, unwilling to believe what he has to say.

—*Allen Sinai (1939–), American economist*

TESTING FOR IMPAIRMENT IS THE largest single conceptual difference between U.S. Generally Accepted Accounting Principles (GAAP) and International Financial Reporting Standards (IFRS). Since 2001 GAAP has had a pair of two-step tests. The first, for long-lived assets (ASC 360, *Property, Plant and Equipment*), is applied to individual items both physical and intangible; the second relates to goodwill in reporting units (ASC 350, *Intangibles—Goodwill and Other*). IFRS, since 1998, has less complexity with a single-step test in International Accounting Standard (IAS) 36, *Impairment of Assets.* This is applied either to an asset or, for goodwill, to one or a group of cash-generating units (CGUs). This chapter deals first with reporting units, then cash-generating units, followed by examples of the two impairment testing processes under GAAP and, between them, for a single asset under IFRS.

REPORTING UNITS

The concept of a reporting unit is essential to the application of both GAAP impairment tests. Under ASC 805, *Business Combinations,* all assets (financial, physical, and intangible) acquired and liabilities assumed in an asset purchase or business combination, as well as the resulting goodwill, must be allocated to a reporting unit. This is either a functional or geographic operating segment established under ASC 280, *Segment Reporting,* or a component of one. Any activity satisfying one of the following is both an operating segment and a reporting unit:

1. It represents 10% or more of total sales to both external customers and other reporting units.
2. It has a reported profit or loss of 10% or more of the greater of (a) the combined profits of all operating segments that did not incur a loss, or (b) the combined losses of all activities that did so.
3. It holds 10% or more of the combined assets of all operating segments.

When Does a Component Become a Reporting Unit?

Whether or not a component is a reporting unit is a matter of judgment based on the individual facts and circumstances. It is a separate reporting unit if: (1) it constitutes a business for which discrete financial information is available, (2) it is subject to regular review by segment management, and (3) it has dissimilar economic characteristics. An operating segment is a single reporting unit if: (1) all of its components are similar, (2) none of its components is considered a reporting unit, or (3) it comprises only one component.

The determination does not depend on any single factor or characteristic. How an entity manages its operations and how a target is integrated with the acquirer (purchaser) has considerable impact in establishing the appropriate reporting units. When the business is managed by product line, the reporting units are organized the same way. If it is managed geographically, the reporting units reflect this and goodwill is allocated to those units that benefit from it.

Whether a component is a business also involves judgment; for a transferred set of activities and assets to be a business, it must contain all of the inputs and processes necessary for it to continue to conduct normal operations after the transaction.

In general, the assessment should be more qualitative than quantitative; the fact that an activity results in revenues and expenses does not mean that it is a business; it might be a product line or a brand that is merely part of a business. When one component extensively shares assets and resources with others, it is likely either not a separate business or economically similar to them. However, components that have similar economic characteristics but are part of different operating segments may not be combined into a single reporting unit.

For example, an entity might be organized geographically into three operating segments (Americas, Europe, and Asia); if each has both manufacturing and service components, the entity would not be permitted to combine similar operations from more than one operating segment to create a reporting unit. If one or more of their components are economically dissimilar, they are likely to be separate reporting units.

Determination Process

The process of determining reporting units begins with selecting operating segments and then disaggregating economically dissimilar components. The focus of ASC 350 is on how the reporting units, rather than the entity as a whole, are managed. Under it a "segment manager is directly accountable to and maintains regular contact with the chief operating decision maker to discuss operating activities, financial results, forecasts or plans for the segment." There is no requirement that management be accountable or have constant contact, but merely must regularly review the results. Therefore, many components aggregated into operating segments are separate reporting units, especially if they are not economically similar.

Assets and liabilities are allocated to a reporting unit if they relate to its operations and would be taken into consideration in assessing its fair value. In an entity with more than one reporting unit, items that do not meet these conditions, such as a headquarters building, environmental liabilities from a discontinued business, or corporate debt, need not be allocated, but may be treated as corporate assets. Pension liabilities are integral to the workforce and have to be allocated, as are taxes, adjusted for consolidated returns.

Most management adopts the same techniques to identify reporting units as for operating segments. Those organized geographically may have difficulties in allocating goodwill when some have several distinct businesses. In such cases, if the operations have not been subsumed into other activities, the legal entities in which the goodwill was recorded on acquisition are the relevant reporting units. While, for simplicity, most managements prefer the segment level for reporting units, in practice it is usually necessary to have a combination of segments and components.

 ## CASH-GENERATING UNITS

The cash-generating unit (CGU) is fundamental to the IFRS impairment testing process. One of the most difficult tasks of IFRS adoption is the identification of the relevant CGUs; fortunately, they are generally not a factor for depreciation, depletion, or amortization. A CGU is based solely on cash inflows, defined as "the smallest identifiable group of assets that generates cash inflows that are largely independent of the cash inflows from other assets or groups of assets." This is a significantly lower level than a reporting unit or even a cost center; for a retail chain, it is undoubtedly each individual store. A CGU cannot be larger than an operating segment, which is effectively the same rule as for GAAP.

Selecting CGUs is done by a bottom-up method considering relevant factors in parallel, rather than sequentially, using aggregation where possible. For impairment testing, goodwill and corporate assets are allocated to various CGUs on a reasonable, auditable basis, applied consistently. If it is not possible to accurately allocate assets to independent CGUs, the level chosen is likely to be too low. The definition is key to CGU identification, although other factors, set out in the following list, may assist in determining whether the cash inflows are largely independent:

- Is the individual asset's or CGU's activity largely independent of other assets or activities and significant to the business?
- How does management monitor the unit's operations or make decisions regarding the continuation or disposition of its assets/operations?
- Is there a shared or common infrastructure?
- Do any activities (e.g., transportation) operate independently in a particular area?
- Are any intermediate products, such as tubing, produced that may have an active market, even if it is all used internally?
- Are there outside users of the infrastructure, such as subleased space?
- Are the CGUs a reasonable basis for allocating assets or activities?

- Do regulatory requirements result in needing a separate entity in a particular area?
- Is financial information readily available at the level selected?

The ability to sell an asset on a stand-alone basis may be indicative of an independent cash inflow. One or a group of assets with independent cash inflows (for example, a printing press and peripherals) that share cash outflows (e.g., labor) with other assets still could be a CGU depending on the degree of shared infrastructures. The choices should represent how the business is organized, be meaningful to investors, reflect operational integration of business units, consider shared facilities, have a consistent definition, and allocate corporate assets on a reasonable, supportable basis.

Examples

A mining enterprise owns a private railway (separately incorporated for regulatory purposes) to support its iron ore activities. It is used mainly to transport the ore with a single passenger car for staff and mail. It does not generate significant revenue, as the mine pays all expenses on a cost-plus basis. The railway could be sold only for scrap and does not generate cash inflows that are largely independent of those from the mine; therefore it is not a CGU.

A bus company provides services under contract with a municipality that requires minimum services on five separate routes. Assets devoted to each route and the relevant cash flow can be separately identified. One route operates at a significant loss; except for materiality, each route would be a separate CGU. ▪

GOODWILL

Under GAAP and IFRS, goodwill is the excess of the cost of an acquired entity over the net of the amounts (fair values) assigned to the assets acquired and liabilities assumed. The amount recognized as goodwill includes acquired intangible assets that do not meet the criteria in ASC 805 or IAS 38 for recognition apart from goodwill. This implies that goodwill has at least five components:

1. Fair values of net items acquired but not recorded as intangible assets in the purchase price allocation (PPA)
2. Fair value of the target's going-concern element

3. Fair value of the synergies expected from combining the businesses
4. Overpayment or underpayment by the acquirer
5. Fair value of the assembled workforce.

ALLOCATIONS

The key to allocating assets and liabilities to reporting or cash-generating units is proper identification. Assets and liabilities are assigned if they are employed in or related to its operations, or would be considered in determining its fair value. Most enterprises allocate the assets and liabilities of a target to more than one unit pro rata on the basis of either benefits expected to be received or their relative fair values. A common technique is to apply intercompany charges; an office building used by more than one unit may be allocated to the occupant of the largest portion, with rent charged to the others. This technique can also be applied to the assets and liabilities of shared services.

Problems may arise when an asset, such as a brand name or customer list, is important to more than one unit. One solution is allocation on the basis of relevant sales, perhaps averaged over a period. Assets and liabilities that reside within a unit that is a separate legal entity but do not relate to its operations, such as future income tax benefits, normally remain. All goodwill from an acquisition is assigned to those units that are expected to benefit from the anticipated synergies, even if the other assets or liabilities of the target are allocated differently. Goodwill does not relate solely to the corporate entity acquired, but to reporting or cash-generating units.

When the fair values of the identifiable net assets acquired in a business combination exceed the fair value of the consideration transferred plus any noncontrolling interest in the target, it is a bargain purchase. In such rare cases, the acquirer recognizes that excess as a gain attributable to the transaction. FASB believes this improves the faithfulness and completeness of information about the acquirer's earnings during the bargain purchase and the measurement of assets obtained.

GAAP LONG-LIVED ASSETS IMPAIRMENT TEST

Under ASC 360, long-lived physical and intangible assets are tested for impairment by a two-step process that is different from that for goodwill. The first determines the potential for impairment; the second measures the loss. It must be completed and any write-off recorded before the GAAP goodwill impairment test may be undertaken. Step 1 does not require determining the fair value of an asset or a group of assets; it merely compares each carrying amount with the undiscounted cash flows the item is expected to generate. Step 2 measures the impairment loss as the difference between the fair value, normally obtained by discounting its projected cash flows, and the carrying amount.

Example

A major intangible asset owned by many companies is its core technology. Due to innovations by both the entity and its competitors, this has a relatively short life, usually between three and seven years, depending on the nature of the business, the amount of R&D involved, and the degree of protection, such as patents or copyrights. In our example most of the value is in a patent, with a remaining useful life of five years. To determine the fair value of such an asset, the relief-from-royalty method is applied.

At the effective date, based on searches of publicly available databases, owners of similar technologies required royalties of between 2.8% and 4.5% of sales; management decided to choose the median of 3.25%. During the last complete fiscal year, 5.1% of revenues was spent on R&D, confirming the selection. Table 14.1 indicates both the undiscounted and the discounted cash flows projected to be derived from the technology over its remaining useful life.

TABLE 14.1 Cash Flows for Asset Impairment Test ($ thousands)

Year to August 31	2010 Actual	2011 Budget	2012 Forecast	2013 Forecast	2014 Forecast	2015 Forecast
Sales	87,488	83,115	80,650	82,000	86,000	93,650
Growth rate		−5.0%	−3.0%	1.7%	4.9%	8.9%
Portion using technology	60%	48%	33%	25%	18%	15%
Related revenues	52,493	39,895	26,615	20,500	15,480	14,048
Applicable royalty (3.25%)	1,706	1,297	865	666	503	457
Effective date adjustment	—	(324)	—	—	—	—
Derived cash flows	1,706	972	865	666	503	457
Total derived cash flows	3,463 (ex 2010)					
Present value factor (20.0%)		0.8696	0.7246	0.6039	0.5032	0.4194
Discounted cash flows		846	627	402	253	191
Total discounted cash flows	2,319					

(continued)

At the applicable royalty, the total undiscounted derived cash flows are $3,463,000, while their fair value—discounted at 20%—is $2,319,000. If the carrying amount ($2,945,000) is less than the undiscounted cash flows, there is no impairment. However, if it is greater, say $3,500,000, there is a possible impairment and Step 2 is applied to measure the loss. This is not just the $37,000 (1.1%) difference between the carrying amount and the undiscounted figure, but $1,181,000 (33.7%), the excess over the discounted amount, which represents fair value. ■

IFRS IMPAIRMENT TEST

The procedures in IAS 36 are completely different from those of GAAP, as they are applied to all assets in the CGU. IAS 36 involves two specialized concepts—recoverable amount and value in use (VIU). The former is the greater of an asset's fair value less costs to sell (FVLCS), sometimes called the net selling price, or its VIU. The VIU is the discounted present value of the future cash flows expected to arise from the continuing use of the asset and its disposal at the end of its useful life; it uses the entity's own expectations rather than those of market participants that underlie fair values and hence FVLCS.

Fair Value Less Costs to Sell

If either FVLCS or VIU is more than the carrying amount, it is not necessary to calculate the other, as the asset is not impaired. If FVLCS cannot be easily determined, then the recoverable amount is the VIU. For assets to be sold, the recoverable amount is the FVLCS. When there is a binding sale agreement, the FVLCS is that price less disposal costs. If there is an active market for the type of asset, the market price (current bid if available, otherwise that of the most recent transaction), less selling costs, is used. If there is no active market, FVLCS is the best estimate of the asset's selling price less direct, additional disposal costs, excluding existing expenses and overheads. When possible, the recoverable amount is determined for each individual asset. If it is not practical to determine it for a particular asset, it is calculated for a group of related assets or for the CGU in which the item is held.

The FVLCS of the technologies is the discounted amount obtained by the relief-from-royalty method ($2,319,000), less estimated costs to sell. The latter comprises any commissions or other direct added costs and is normally about

10% of the proceeds. Therefore, the FVLCS at a maximum would be $2,087,000 ($2,319,000 less $232,000). As this is less than the carrying amount of $2,945,000, the VIU must be calculated.

Value in Use

The standard states that the calculation of VIU should reflect:

- Estimates of the future cash flows the entity expects to derive from the asset
- Expectations about possible variations in their amount or timing
- The time value of money, represented by the current market risk-free rate of interest
- The price for bearing the uncertainty inherent in the asset
- Other factors, such as illiquidity that market participants would reflect in pricing the expected future cash flows

Cash flow projections should be based on reasonable and supportable assumptions and the most recent budgets and forecasts (normally for five years), with extrapolations for later periods. Management can assess the reasonableness of its assumptions by examining the causes of differences between past cash flow projections and the actual results. VIU relates to the asset in its current condition; future restructurings to which the entity is not committed and expenditures to improve or enhance its performance should not be anticipated. The projections for a VIU do not include any cash inflows or outflows from financing activities, nor income tax receipts or payments; therefore all calculations are pretax.

Discount Rate

In measuring VIU, the discount rate applied is the pretax level that reflects current market assessments of the time value of money and the risks specific to the asset; those reflected in the cash flows are excluded. The objective is a rate of return that investors would require if they were to choose an equally risky investment that generates cash flows equivalent to those expected from the asset.

For an individual asset, group of assets, or CGU, the discount rate is that which the entity would pay in a current market transaction to borrow money to buy that specific item. If a market-determined item-specific rate is not available, a surrogate is developed reflecting the time value of money over the asset's life, as well as relevant country (location), currency, price, and cash flow risks.

A valuator normally considers the entity's weighted average cost of capital (WACC), its incremental borrowing rate, and other market lending rates for similar credits.

For the first five years, the derived cash flows for the VIU of the technology are the same as those established for GAAP, with an extrapolation for the next four years during which benefits are expected from the fully amortized asset. However, the discount rate is not necessarily the same.

While WACC and other market-derived discount rates are after tax, VIU requires the pretax level. With WACC of 9.8%, the applicable discount rate is possibly less than the 20% used to calculate the fair value, since, based on a 33% tax rate, the pretax cost of equity is only 17.1%.

One way to obtain this is to first determine a proxy VIU as the after-tax present value at the cost of equity. The pretax discount rate that gives the same result is then estimated; in this case, it is 33.25%. However, management decided that the appropriate rate is between 20% and 25%. Those give a VIU between $2,500,000 (25%) and $2,725,000 (20%); the selected amount is $2,600,000, which is also the recoverable amount as it is the greater of the FVLCS ($2,087,000) and the VIU. As this is less than the carrying amount ($2,945,000), there is an impairment loss of the difference ($345,000). In general, the IFRS test results in frequent small impairment charges rather than a few large ones.

Reversal of Impairment Losses

When there is an indication that an impairment loss for an asset may have decreased, the related recoverable amount is calculated, and if that exceeds the current carrying amount, the latter may be increased by reversing a previous impairment charge. There is no reversal for unwinding of discounts. The increased carrying amount due to a reversal should not be more than what the depreciated historical cost would have been if the impairment had not been recognized. Such a reversal is recognized as income, and depreciation for future periods adjusted. Reversals of losses on goodwill impairments are prohibited.

 GAAP GOODWILL IMPAIRMENT TEST

To determine if any goodwill is impaired, GAAP applies a different two-step process at the reporting unit, rather than at the asset level. Again, Step 1

identifies potential impairments and Step 2 measures the amount, if any, of the loss. The test is required at least once a year on the same date, which does not have to be the year-end; each reporting unit may choose its own date. In addition, it is required when one of the following occurs, if the event is likely to reduce the fair value of the reporting unit:

- There is a significant adverse change in a legal situation or in the business climate.
- There is an adverse action or assessment by a regulator.
- An unanticipated competitor enters the market.
- Key personnel leave the firm.
- Consideration is given to the possible sale or disposition of all or a significant portion of a reporting unit.
- An impairment test under ASC 360 results in a write-off.
- A subsidiary that is part of a reporting unit recognizes an impairment loss.

Step 1 of the GAAP goodwill test determines if there is a potential impairment by comparing the fair value of the reporting unit with its carrying amount. If the fair value is greater, there is no impairment and no further action is required. If the carrying amount exceeds the fair value, then Step 2 is undertaken. It measures the impairment loss for a reporting unit to which it is applied by comparing the implied fair value of that goodwill to its carrying amount. If it is higher, there is no charge. If it is lower, a goodwill impairment loss has to be recorded.

The implied fair value of a reporting unit's goodwill is determined in the same manner as in a PPA, with an assumed purchase price of the fair value. It requires identifying and establishing the fair values of all financial, physical, and intangible assets as well as liabilities, including unrecorded intangible assets that were internally generated, acquired in a pooling transaction, or previously formed part of goodwill; common examples are core technologies, customer lists, and brands.

FASB believes that goodwill cannot be valued directly and that its fair value must be obtained as a residual. Therefore, under Step 2, the implied fair value of the goodwill is the difference between that of the reporting unit as a whole and the total of the fair values of all identified assets, less those of the liabilities.

Example

Consider a typical reporting unit, as shown in Table 14.2.

TABLE 14.2 Step 2 of GAAP Goodwill Impairment Test ($ thousands)

	Carrying Amounts	Fair Value	Difference
Assets			
Current	5,346	6,058	712
Property, plant & equipment	1,047	2,031	984
Intangible assets	3,795	2,042	(1,753)
Unrecorded intangibles	—	1,055	1,055
Total	10,188	11,186	998
Liabilities			
Current	3,112	2,782	(330)
Term	3,276	3,487	211
Total	6,388	6,269	(119)
Net assets	3,800	4,917	1,117
Equity	9,125	9,000	(125)
Net assets	(3,800)	(4,917)	(1,117)
Goodwill	5,325	4,083	(1,242)

In this example, which for simplicity ignores all tax effects, the fair value of the equity ($9,000,000) is less than its carrying amount ($9,125,000). Therefore, Step 2 of the goodwill impairment test has to be applied, which requires determining the fair values of all assets and liabilities. The sources of the differences are shown in Table 14.3. The result of restating all assets and liabilities is an implied fair value of $4,083,000 for the goodwill. As its carrying amount is $5,325,000, the impairment loss is $1,242,000, the excess over the implied fair value. One reason the impairment loss is greater than the reduction in the equity ($125,000) is because Step 2 includes unrecorded, internally generated intangible assets amounting to $1,055,000.

TABLE 14.3 Step 2 of GAAP Goodwill Impairment Test ($ thousands)

	Sources of Differences	
Assets		
Current	105	Unrealized gain on marketable securities
	607	Last in, first out inventory reserve
Total	712	
Property, plant & equipment	1,062	Excess of appraised value of plant's real state over net book values
	(78)	Difference between resale amounts for computer equipment and net book value
Total	984	
Intangible assets	1,753	Difference between their fair values using the discounted cash flow method, allocated on the basis of current sales over the amortized carrying amounts, recorded according to preacquisition sales
Unrecorded intangibles	1,055	Fair value, using a DCF method, of internally generated brand, allocated by current sales
Liabilities		
Current	(330)	Reversal of accruals no longer required
Term	211	Term loan is at 8.5% with 63 remaining monthly payments of $52,000 each; the difference is the excess, over the current balance, of total future payments of principal and interest, discounted over the remaining term at the present rate of 6% a year (0.485% a month).
Equity	(125)	The fair value of the reporting unit based on both the market (guideline entities) and the income (DCF value) approaches is $9,000,000, while the carrying amount is $9,125,000.

Application

This process of allocating fair values relates solely to the goodwill impairment test and does not lead to changes in any carrying amounts. In particular, internally generated intangibles, whose fair values are included in Step 2, are not reflected. The only adjustment made is to reduce the recorded goodwill by the impairment loss, which may not exceed its carrying amount. After the impairment loss is applied, goodwill is always reported at this lower level, which is its new accounting basis in the future. GAAP does not permit subsequent reversals of previously recognized impairment losses. Impairment loss cannot be avoided by reorganizing reporting units that are dependent on the managerial structure of the entity.

Market Capitalization

In assessing the fair value of a reporting or cash-generating unit, publicly traded entities must consider their overall market capitalization; this should reconcile, within a reasonable range, to the total of the fair values of the individual units. This is a means of ascertaining whether the aggregate estimated equity values for all its units is supported by market participants' perspectives; a higher total may be justified by a control premium or synergies. Given market conditions from 2007 to 2009, an entity should consider trends in its trading prices rather than merely relying on a single day's closing figure.

CHAPTER FIFTEEN

The Auditor's Blessing

Facts and truth don't have much to do with each other.

—*William Faulkner (1897–1962), American author*

NOW WE COME TO THE LAST CHAPTER, dealing with the role of the auditor in blessing all the estimates of fair value found in a set of financial statements. Those amounts involve all kinds of assets and many types of markets, ranging from the most liquid, such as U.S. Treasury bills, notes, or bonds, to the merely notional, composed of potential market participants. My comments draw on several documents from the organizations creating the standards that govern audit procedures; they are the International Federation of Accountants, which issues the International Standards on Auditing (ISA) and the American Institute of Certified Public Accountants, the source of (U.S.) Statements on Auditing Standards (SAS). Under the standards, auditors are expected to be aware of, and completely understand, the principles and rules relating to the measurement, accounting, and disclosure of fair values, which are of growing importance in many financial reporting frameworks.

Credit crunches and reduced market liquidity during the recent Great Recession (2008–) have highlighted the difficulties that arise in valuing assets, especially financial instruments, when suitable information either is not available or is difficult to obtain. Many national and international regulatory and other organizations have tried to assist users, preparers, and auditors of financial statements to deal with these problems. However, the best available auditable evidence from valuators and management, together with experienced judgment on the part of auditors, is the only satisfactory solution.

Particularly relevant for readers are the procedures and tests applied by auditors in evaluating whether the significant assumptions used to measure the fair values, individually and taken as a whole, provide a reasonable basis for including their conclusions in the entity's financial statements. Since these tests must be applied by the auditor, they should prudently have already been addressed by management, as assumptions go to the heart of financial projections. The key is to confirm that the assumptions are reasonable and they reflect, or at least are consistent with, information believed to be used by market participants. Another test of the reliability of management's valuation processes is to compare the results in the current period with those determined previously, taking into account changes in market or economic conditions.

AUDITING FAIR VALUES

Fair value measurements differ from other accounting estimates because, when market prices are not available, management must obtain a supportable figure using an appropriate technique and assumptions that reflect those of outsiders—market participants. This unique characteristic, combined with the numerous standards involving valuations, the complexity of some methods, and their significance to financial statements, makes the task of auditing them difficult. While every situation will inevitably be different from others and, in some cases, circumstances may affect the valuation process, there are a few characteristics of a valuation report that the auditor will need in order to find it acceptable. In particular it should:

▪ *Be well-documented.* The auditor should be able to follow the processes step-by-step. All supporting documentation used by management or a valuator should be clearly listed with copies available in the working papers. It is essential that the narrative is sufficiently detailed so that all the approaches, methods, and techniques considered and used are easily understood.

▪ *Demonstrate knowledge of all relevant facts and circumstances.* If the auditor is not aware of pertinent facts relating to the entity, he or she will be unable to provide a reasonable conclusion. Unless the report demonstrates this, the auditor will be unable to rely on it.

▪ *Make sense.* The objective is a document written in clear, concise language reflecting the existing economic situation and providing evidence, preferably market-based, for each significant assumption, conjecture, or judgment.

In addition, it must fully define the assignment, including the following:

▪ *Objective:* Specifying the client, the business, and the items to be valued
▪ *Purpose:* Why the assignment was undertaken, such as to comply with GAAP or IFRS
▪ *Effective date:* The relevant measurement date
▪ *Standard of value:* The definition of fair value adopted by GAAP and IFRS
▪ *Scope and limitations:* Specifying the information relied on and what the report does and does not purport to do

The following content is particularly important in auditing estimates of fair value:

▪ The objective, as the conclusions relate to real or hypothetical current transactions in financial statement items, based on conditions prevalent at a particular date
▪ The extent to which judgments and significant assumptions have been made by those other than management, such as experts engaged by the entity or employed by the auditor
▪ The availability or absence of information or evidence and its reliability
▪ The range of assets and liabilities for which fair values are being estimated
▪ The choice and sophistication of the valuation techniques and models adopted
▪ The information for appropriate disclosure about measurement methods and uncertainty, especially when the relevant markets are illiquid or imaginary

Challenges

In the current (2011) environment, one of the greatest difficulties faced by preparers of financial statements, and consequently auditors, is obtaining reliable relevant information to determine fair values. The nature and the reliability of the supporting material vary widely, as do the associated uncertainties. When markets become inactive or illiquid, transaction data may be inadequate or unavailable and fair values have to be estimated on the basis of other, often unobservable information, frequently using models. This increases the auditor's potential doubts and raises concerns about the risks of material misstatements.

What appears to management to be a routine valuation may to the auditor be a source of significant risks. In such circumstances, the entity should endeavor to minimize any limits on the information that management possesses or can obtain, and should make everything available as potential audit evidence. Auditors require adequate, appropriate, supporting information for all significant inputs or assumptions used by management. Those include the experience and expertise of the personnel involved, what relevant market information was identified and used, and how changes in the assumptions were monitored. Experience indicates that, while estimates of fair values are sometimes extremely difficult to determine in times of market uncertainty, if they are properly prepared, it is usually possible to obtain sufficient information to allow the auditor to bless recording the final figures in the financial statements.

As discussed in previous chapters, fair values apply to many more items than financial assets or liabilities. Depending on the reporting framework, they may affect management's determinations of pension liabilities, recorded amounts for goodwill and intangible assets acquired in business combinations, real estate, endowment funds, share-based payments, nonmonetary exchanges, and many other items.

Audit Requirements

The principal, directly relevant standard is ISA 545, *Auditing Fair Value Measurements and Disclosures*. Fair value measurements of assets, liabilities, and components of equity are needed both on their initial recording and later, reflecting all subsequent changes. In addition, financial instruments and other assets recorded at historical cost often require fair value conclusions for supplementary disclosure in the notes to the financial statements or in estimating provisions or impairment losses. Changes in fair values that occur over time are treated in various ways under different reporting frameworks; some reflect them directly in equity, whereas others require their recording as income.

The standard (ISA 545) sets out an overarching obligation for the auditor to obtain sufficient appropriate evidence to confirm that the fair value measurements and disclosures are in accordance with the entity's applicable reporting framework. Additional provisions modify the requirements of other standards to cover auditing fair values; in particular they deal with understanding the entity and its environment, risks of material misstatements, using the work of an expert, management representations, communication with the directors, disclosures, possible fraud, and going concern.

Understanding the Entity and Its Environment

For any engagement, an auditor is required to obtain a detailed understanding of the entities involved and the environment in which they operate. This involves reviewing the internal controls in sufficient detail to identify and assess the risks of material misstatement of the financial statements whether due to error or to fraud. Such a review will include understanding the entities' objectives and strategies, knowledge of the process for identifying business risks relevant to financial reporting, and procedures for deciding how to address them.

When a purchase price allocation is involved, the discussion in the valuation report related to the target should disclose sufficient knowledgeable of its assets, liabilities, revenues, and expenses that the auditor is satisfied that adequate due diligence was undertaken to support the value conclusions; it should also mention any characteristics of either company that play a material role in the valuation process. The description of the target should include its history, businesses, and structure; the competitive environment; and key operational considerations.

Past financial performance provides an important context for the acquirer's plans. While projected cash flows are the most relevant to the fair values of the assets acquired and the liabilities assumed, the target's historical performance is a useful tool to substantiate the reasonableness of the projections. This does not mean that a firm that has never made money cannot normally be expected to operate profitably in the future; it signifies that management must have a compelling growth or turnaround story thoroughly explained in the valuation report.

Valuation Processes

Management is responsible for establishing the projection, valuation, accounting, and financial reporting processes for all fair value measurements. In some cases, when published prices are available, the measurement, and therefore the process, may be simple and reliable. Other measurements, however, are inherently more elaborate and may involve significant assumptions, particularly if there are no active markets. A complete understanding of the processes, including all the significant and complex assumptions plus their degree of subjectivity, helps an auditor identify and assess the risks involved.

Many financial institutions have established rigorous valuation processes and make detailed disclosures. Comprehensive internal processes requiring critical judgment and discipline in valuing holdings of complex or illiquid assets have assisted many of them in dealing with the challenges of certain markets. Therefore auditors, as part of understanding the relevant industry and regulatory factors, usually ask management about any discussions with regulators about valuation practices, and when it last revised its own processes.

Specific Assets

Due to the sophisticated nature of certain financial instruments, it is vital that both the entity and the auditor completely understand the securities in which the entity has invested or to which it is exposed, as well as the related risks. The auditor's understanding is often obtained by reviewing the processes for investing in particular instruments and the information relied on in making those decisions.

Intangible assets are an important part of most business combinations, yet discussions in the PPA valuation report are often the first information the auditor obtains about them. Therefore, the report should give both detailed descriptions and indications of their significance to the valuation. A helpful addition is an overview of the relevant technical accounting guidance demonstrating awareness of the applicable standards and acceptable valuation methods. This section should clearly indicate how the various intangible assets contribute to the value of the entity, especially their impacts on cash flows, risks, and growth.

Risks of Material Misstatements

The nature, timing, and extent of the auditor's procedures depend on the susceptibility to misstatement of each fair value measurement. The practices adopted are based on the risks involved, as reflected partly by the answers to the following questions:

* What control procedures are in place for making investment decisions?
* How are those decisions communicated with the directors?
* What level of due diligence is associated with each particular investment?
* Did management evaluate the risks from each asset before investing?
* What is the expertise of those responsible for making investment decisions?

- Has the entity the ability to subsequently value the assets involved?
- Is there appropriate segregation between the individuals responsible for making investments and those determining their values?
- Has management a track record in assessing the risks of particular types of investment instruments?

Difficulties may exist when fair value estimates require unobservable inputs; in particular, management may not have the internal expertise to value illiquid or complex financial or technological assets, and the available information may be limited. Therefore, it is often necessary to make assumptions, including those based on the work of an expert, to develop such fair values. Assumptions are integral to many valuation methods—for example, those that discount to the present a combination of projected cash flows and an estimate of the value of the item at a future date.

The reliability of supporting information is influenced by its source and nature. Management may use dealer quotes to support the fair value of a financial investment or material investment; however, when it is from the firm that initially sold the asset, the evidence may be subjective and need supplementing from one or more alternative sources, such as a pricing service, many of which unfortunately use undisclosed valuation methods. To assess such information, the auditor must obtain an understanding of how it is developed. Is it based on private trades? Deals in similar assets? A cash flow model? Some combination of inputs? Inquiries into the nature of a quotation are directed at its reliability and adherence to the objective and definition of fair value.

Choice of Methods

Changes in markets may affect the choice of valuation methods; consistency is generally a desirable quality in financial information, but possibly inappropriate if circumstances change. An example in ISA 545 shows how the introduction of an active market might result in a market-based fair value replacing a model-based one; past changes have tended to be in the opposite direction as markets became inactive. Even when a model has been consistently applied, the appropriateness of the underlying assumptions needs periodic review. One that was calibrated when adequate market information was available may not provide reasonable conclusions in a time of market stress. Consequently, the consistency of valuation methods or assumptions and the appropriateness of changes are of concern to auditors. Such changes do not alter the underlying measurement objective, which is fair value as defined.

Audit Evidence

Guidance on audit evidence, the quantity and quality needed, and the procedures to obtain it are set out in ISA 500, *Audit Evidence*. The term is defined as "all of the information used by the auditor in arriving at the conclusions on which the audit opinion is based." Unless management is able to adequately support its fair values, it is difficult for the auditor to obtain sufficient appropriate audit evidence. However, information underlying the assumptions and the validity of models is necessarily less reliable than an actual price in an active market.

It is therefore often necessary to look at additional sources to accumulate enough appropriate material; the greater the risk of misstatement, the more audit evidence is required. For example, an auditor, or his or her expert, seeking to determine if management's conclusions are reasonable, may compare the results of an independent model with those of the model used by management. Auditors may also consider whether external sources provide additional evidence to benchmark the entity's practices; sources that track transactions by financial institutions may provide evidence as to the reasonableness of an entity's fair values for similar investments.

General Audit Procedures

Guidance on auditing fair values in financial statements is also provided by SAS 101, *Auditing Fair Values*. This states that management is responsible for fair value measurements, establishing the necessary accounting and financial reporting processes, choosing appropriate valuation methods, identifying and adequately supporting all significant assumptions, preparing the valuation report, and ensuring that the presentation and disclosures reflect GAAP or IFRS as the case may be; these obligations apply even when an accredited valuation specialist is retained.

The audit procedures are intended to assist the auditor in:

- Gaining sufficient understanding of the entity's valuation processes, relevant controls, and the role of information technology
- Considering the extent to which management relied on experts
- Assessing inherent and control risks
- Evaluating whether the conclusions are in accordance with GAAP or IFRS
- Considering the significance of management's assumptions
- Obtaining evidence, when relevant, as to management's intent and ability to carry out specific courses of action regarding significant assumptions
- Evaluating management's choice of valuation methods adopted, and whether they are appropriate when alternatives are available

■ Assessing whether the entity's valuation processes have been consistently applied

The auditor will perform at least the following mandatory procedures:

■ Test the entity's processes by reviewing the significant assumptions, any valuation models, plus the related documentation and information.
■ Evaluate whether the significant assumptions, taken individually and as a whole, provide a reasonable basis for the conclusions.
■ Test the data used to develop the fair values and confirm they have been properly obtained from the data using management's assumptions.
■ Verify the sources of data, confirm the mathematical calculations, and review the relevant information for internal consistency.
■ Determine to what extent management used available market information to develop its assumptions.
■ Develop independent estimates of fair values to corroborate the appropriateness of the entity's measurements, using sensitivity analysis.
■ Evaluate the sufficiency and appropriateness of the audit evidence obtained, and its consistency with other evidence gathered during the audit.
■ Consider which matters should be communicated with the directors.
■ Confirm both the intent and the ability of management to carry out specific courses of action when they are relevant to fair values.

Verifying Significant Assumptions

As the auditor will focus his attention on important assumptions, identifying those that appear to be significant to the fair values requires the exercise of judgment by management. Generally, significant assumptions cover matters that materially affect the fair value measurements and include those that are sensitive to variation or uncertainty in amount or nature, or susceptible to misapplication or bias. For example, those about short-term interest rates tend to be less susceptible to major variations than are assumptions about long-term rates. Specific assumptions will vary with the characteristics of the asset or liability being valued and the valuation approach—market, cost, or income—adopted. When a discounted cash flows method under the income approach is used, the assumptions about the amounts of the cash flows, the projection period, the terminal amount, and the discount rate are all considered significant.

The sensitivity of each fair value to changes in significant assumptions, including market conditions, will also be considered by an auditor. Normally management will apply techniques like sensitivity analysis to identify particularly susceptible assumptions. If it has not done such procedures, the auditor will usually undertake the task herself as part of her review of the assumptions, individually and taken as a whole, to determine whether they are reasonable, realistic, supported by adequate audit evidence, and consistent with:

- The general economic environment and the entity's economic circumstances
- Existing market information
- The entity's plans, including management's expectations about the outcome of specific objectives and strategies
- Assumptions that were made in previous periods, if appropriate
- Past experience of, or previous conditions experienced by, the entity to the extent currently applicable
- Assumptions used by management in preparing other accounting estimates
- Risks associated with projected cash flows, including potential variability and any related effect on the discount rate
- The nature of the appropriate valuation model adopted
- The entity's actual plans and past experience

Subsequent Events

The auditor considers the effect of subsequent events on the fair values; if there are any, the relevant audit standards apply. Fair values are measured as of a specific time; while hindsight is clearly inadmissible, events and transactions that occur after that date but before the completion of fieldwork, such as the sale of an investment shortly afterward, may provide evidence regarding its fair value. Some subsequent events or transactions reflect changes in circumstances and thus are not evidence of fair value. When using a subsequent event or transaction to substantiate a fair value, the auditor considers only events or transactions that reflect circumstances at the valuation date.

Level 3 Inputs

Level 3 of the hierarchy, referred to in previous chapters, contemplates estimating fair values based on financial projections, such as for a discounted cash flows method; such cases are characterized by greater uncertainty regarding the reliability of the measurement process resulting from:

- The length of the forecast period
- The number of significant and complex assumptions adopted

- A degree of subjectivity associated with the assumptions and factors used
- Uncertainties associated with the future occurrence or outcome of events underlying the assumptions employed
- Lack of objective data when highly subjective inputs are used

The auditor will assess all the Level 3 inputs in the light of those factors to confirm that they truly represent the views of market participants, rather than those of management.

Using the Work of an Expert

When auditing financial statements including fair values, it is essential that one or more members of the team are sufficiently skilled and knowledgeable about valuation; to ensure the required quality control, a specialist valuator may also be necessary. The auditor may be aware of this need for expertise when accepting the engagement or later, after having gained an understanding of the entity and its environment. ISA 545 requires the auditor to determine when an expert is needed, and ISA 620, *Using the Work of an Expert*, establishes standards and supplies guidance on using the results as audit evidence, whether the expert was hired by the entity or by the auditor.

Even when using the work of an expert, the auditor has to obtain sufficient appropriate audit evidence to satisfy her purpose. ISA 620 explains that when an expert is used, the appropriateness and reasonableness of assumptions and methods used and their application are the expert's responsibility. However, the auditor needs to obtain a sufficient understanding of the assumptions and methods involved to determine if they are appropriate and reasonable, based on the auditor's knowledge of the business and the results of other audit procedures. In addition, ISA 545 includes guidance on the use of an expert, such as considering that professional's expertise and experience and evaluating whether the data used for the conclusions is accurate and complete.

Management Representations

ISA 545 requires the auditor to obtain written representations from management regarding the reasonableness of significant assumptions, including, when it is relevant to the fair value measurements or disclosures, whether they appropriately reflect management's intent and ability to carry out specific courses of action. Depending on the nature, materiality, and complexity of the fair values contained in the financial statements, management's representations about the measurements and disclosures may also include information about:

- The appropriateness of the measurement methods, including related assumptions used in determining fair values and the consistency in application of the methods
- The appropriateness of the bases used to overcome any presumptions relating to the use of fair values for those accounting estimates not so measured
- The completeness and appropriateness of disclosure related to fair values under the entity's financial reporting framework
- Whether, due to subsequent events, adjustments are needed to any fair value measurements and disclosures included in the financial statements

Communication with the Directors

Effective two-way communication between the auditor and the directors is mandated by ISA 260, *Communication with Those Charged with Governance*. Because of the uncertainties associated with fair value measurements, the potential effects on the financial statements of any significant risks may be of governance interest; examples are the nature of significant assumptions used, the degree of subjectivity involved in their development, and the relative materiality of the items being measured at fair value to the financial statements as a whole. The need for appropriate controls over commitments for financial instruments and their subsequent measurement processes may also give rise to the need for communication.

Certain audit matters of interest to directors are likely to be important to regulators, particularly when they may require urgent action. In many countries, requirements concerning the auditor's communication with regulators are established by law, supervisory requirements, or formal agreements. When there are no such rules, the auditor should encourage management to communicate, on a timely basis, matters that may be of significance to a regulator.

Disclosures

The auditor is required to confirm that the disclosures about fair values are in accordance with the entity's financial reporting framework. In times of uncertainty, disclosures assume greater significance and the auditor may in certain cases regard potential misstatement in disclosures as a significant risk. For example, some financial reporting frameworks prescribe the disclosure of:

- Key assumptions and other sources of estimation uncertainty that have a significant risk of causing a material adjustment to the carrying amounts of assets and liabilities

- The range of possible outcomes and the assumptions used in determining them
- Information regarding the significance of fair value accounting estimates to the entity's reported financial position and performance
- Exposures to risks; how they arise; the objectives, policies, and procedures for managing such risks; methods used to measure them; and any changes from the previous period
- The extent to which the entity is exposed to credit, liquidity, and market risks, based on information available internally to management

Disclosures, although important, do not justify improper accounting or permit management to include fair values in the financial statements without sufficient evidence.

Possible Fraud

ISA 240, *The Auditor's Responsibilities Relating to Fraud*, requires an auditor to consider the risks of material misstatements in the financial statements due to fraud. At times, unexpected losses may arise from extreme fluctuations in commodity or other asset prices or from trading misjudgments, while financing difficulties may create liquidity or solvency pressures. Such situations may motivate fraudulent financial reporting to protect personal bonuses, hide management errors, maintain borrowing capabilities, or avoid reporting losses.

Fraudulent financial reporting often involves management overriding controls that otherwise appear to be operating effectively. This may include, for example, using assumptions for fair values inconsistent with those observable in the marketplace. In illiquid markets, the increased use of models and the lack of market comparisons present opportunities for manipulating or overriding amounts calculated by experts. Even without fraudulent intent, there is a natural temptation to bias judgments toward the most favorable end of what may be a wide spectrum; this is not always the position leading to the highest profit or lowest loss. In auditing fair values, therefore, the auditor will consider whether the circumstances cause increased risks of fraud. In reviewing the judgments and decisions made by management in determining fair values, the auditor may find possible biases; if this is the case, the auditor has to consider the implications for the financial statements as a whole.

Going Concern

An auditor is required to consider whether there are events or conditions and related business risks that may cast significant doubt on the entity's ability to continue as a going concern. An entity is ordinarily viewed as continuing in business for the foreseeable future with neither the intention nor the necessity of liquidation, ceasing trading, or seeking protection from creditors. Accordingly, assets and liabilities are recorded on the basis that the entity will be able to realize its assets and discharge its liabilities in the normal course of business. When faced with deteriorating market conditions, there may be an increased risk of an entity being unable to continue as a going concern. Factors to consider include the effect of:

- Significant adjustments to assets stated at fair values or requiring provisions
- Continued availability of existing sources of finance
- Modifications in the cost and terms of finance
- Changes in markets on the ability to realize assets
- Deteriorating markets in the entity's activities
- Sales of assets at significant losses
- Pending legal or regulatory proceedings

Consideration of those factors may lead the auditor to conclude that a material uncertainty exists relating to the entity's ability to continue as a going concern, which requires disclosure in the financial statements or the auditor's report. ISA 570, *Going Concern*, provides guidance on:

- Active versus inactive markets
- Evaluating available market information
- Using information from brokers and pricing services, including dealers' quotes
- Applying models
- Changes in models and assumptions over time
- Enhanced disclosures about financial instruments of particular interest to readers

 ## CONCLUSION

A lot of work may be required by an auditor to be sufficiently satisfied with management's fair value measurements to bless their inclusion in a set of financial statements. This chapter has described enough of the procedures involved to allow management to accumulate the necessary information to avoid last-minute queries and holdups due to the absence of material.

About the Author

James P. Catty, MA, CPA/ABV (U.S.), CA•CBV (Canada), CVA, CFA, CFE, is president and founder of Corporate Valuation Services Limited (1988), a Canadian firm that specializes in valuing technology-oriented businesses, their securities, and their assets throughout the world. In 2006, he became chairman of the International Association of Consultants, Valuators and Analysts (IACVA), a global financial knowledge transfer and accrediting association with presences in Australia, Canada, China, Germany, Ghana, India, Indonesia, Kenya, Kuwait, Lebanon, Mexico, New Zealand, Nigeria, the Philippines, Russia, Saudi Arabia, South Korea, Taiwan, Thailand, the United States, and Vietnam. Since 2008 he has served as of counsel to Hanlin Moss, PS, Certified Public Accountants of Seattle, United States and Xi'an, China. He holds BA and MA degrees from the University of Oxford and has been active in the profession for over 50 years. His clients range from government departments and agencies to law firms, multinational businesses, local start-ups, and individuals; nearly all are word-of-mouth referrals. He has contributed numerous articles to various publications and made presentations to professional groups in China, France, Germany, Israel, Romania, Taiwan, Turkey, the United Kingdom, and the United States. He is the general editor of *Guide to Fair Value under IFRS*, published by John Wiley & Sons in April 2010, and principal contributor to the first and second editions of the IACVA's training manual, *Business Valuation: Introduction to Intangibles.*

Index

Printed and bound by CPI Group (UK) Ltd, Croydon, CR0 4YY

23/04/2025

14660904-0002